No
BOUNDARIES

MOVING BEYOND SUPPLY CHAIN MANAGEMENT

JAMES A. TOMPKINS, PH.D.

TOMPKINS
PRESS

Library of Congress Cataloging-in-Publication Data

Tompkins, James A.
     No boundaries : moving beyond supply chain
management / James A. Tompkins. -- 1 st. ed.
       p. cm.
     Includes bibliographical references and index.
     LCCN: 00-190121
     ISBN: 0-9658659-2-4

     1. Business logistics. 2. Industrial
productivity. 3. Industrial management.
4. Manufacturing industries--Management.   I. Title.

  HD38.5.T66 2000   658.5
               QBI00-423

ACKNOWLEDGEMENTS

This book has been an exciting endeavor as so much has been happening so quickly. Several people at Tompkins Associates provided valuable support in developing Supply Chain Synthesis and creating this book. Key folks included Bill Stroupe, Jerry Smith, John Spain, Patty Godin, and Rob Haynes.

Of special note is the editorial support and patience of Forsyth Alexander and Brenda Jernigan.

Additionally, the support, love, and patience of my family was key to my being able to finish this work.

Lastly, but also most importantly, has been the support of many of our clients who have allowed us to evolve this work and hatch Supply Chain Synthesis from a good concept to a real, alive, prosperous process. Thanks to all.

James A. Tompkins, Ph.D.
March 11, 2000
Tompkins Associates
Raleigh, North Carolina
jtompkins@tompkinsinc.com

PREFACE

This book began as a search for the science of Supply Chain Management. This search was pursued from a practical perspective working with real clients who had real supply chain challenges. The frustrations, disappointments, and failed Supply Chain Management initiatives were easy to find; impossible to find was the science of Supply Chain Management. This futile search resulted in my understanding the necessity of moving beyond Supply Chain Management and establishing an integrated process for the supply chain.

Tompkins worked with several clients that understood the need for innovation and creativity throughout the supply chain; this allowed us to evolve the integrated supply chain process of Supply Chain Synthesis. This evolution has resulted in many very successful implementations and finally reached the point where it was clear that a book should be written to expound on the science of Supply Chain Synthesis and its impacts on the supply chain.

As I finished the first draft of the book and the publishing people from Tompkins Press got involved, they asked the question about the title of the book. Well, as a Ph.D. engineer who has never had much of a feel for marketing, I thought the book should be called *Supply Chain Synthesis*. Tompkins Press wasn't so sure, so, after a bit of arm twisting, I agreed that we should use a focus group to refine the title of the book. The focus group did not like the title *Supply Chain Synthesis* but very much liked the title *No Boundaries*. I put on my engineer hat, and after reviewing the qualifications of the focus group participants, I concluded that their backgrounds were not sufficient for me to change the title of my book. So, the second writing was done under the enduring title *Supply Chain Synthesis*.

Much to my surprise, the folks of Tompkins Press convened a second focus group on the title of this book. This focus group was staffed with people fully qualified to offer an opinion on the title of this book. Well, you guessed it, they loved the title *No Boundaries* and hated the title *Supply Chain Synthesis*. So, the third writing was done under the banner of *No Boundaries*.

You see, in these days of high customer satisfaction, not even the author of a book can overrule the voice of the customer. So, you asked for it, and I wrote it. Enjoy *No Boundaries*. The journey of the integration, the synthesis of the supply chain begins here.

INTRODUCTION

Supply Chain Management (SCM) has not produced the desired results. SCM has given way to the supply chain fads of Efficient Consumer Response (ECR), Quick Response (QR), and Just-in-Time (JIT) manufacturing and distribution, but the results here too have been disappointing. A 1997 study compiled by the Council of Logistics Management states that the grocery industry actually has more inventory on hand now than it did before SCM and before ECR.

To compound problems, a study compiled by the software developer Manugistics declares that supply chain software is typically used internally to an organization, rather than across the links of the supply chain. This defeats the purpose of software and brings no value to the total supply chain. The customer continues to be dissatisfied.

Slow information. Distorted information. No information. One industry knows the role poor information plays in creating an inefficient supply chain. The Automotive Industry Action Group (AIAG) says that "just in case" inventories associated with information disconnects cost the automotive industry $1 billion annually. Every automobile produced in the United States could cost, on average, $70 less with a better supply chain strategy.

Some believe that the "Information Superhighway" will change all that. Business-to-business (B2B) e-commerce and trade, the revenues of which are supposed to reach well past the $500 billion mark in a year or so, is relying heavily on the Internet to create "communication superhighways" and partnerships. New B2B alliances and partnerships are being formed almost daily; you see the headlines everywhere. These B2B alliances and the systems being built to foster communications between the partners are being hailed as the way to succeed in today's global marketplace. This is only true if the alliance partners discard the traditional relationships fostered by SCM and embrace Supply Chain Synthesis (SCS). One of the eight SCS core competencies is SCS Communications, which has become a reality as the result of the B2B Information Highway. However, SCS Communications is only one of the eight core competencies, and the reality is that your chain must embrace all eight or your chain will not achieve the benefits of SCS. Where we are today with B2B is exactly where we were with ECR in the mid-1990s. ECR relied totally on Electronic Data Interchange (EDI), Automatic Data Collection (AutoID), and Warehouse Management Systems (WMSs) and forgot about the other components to bring about true supply chain excellence. In my 1995 book, *The Genesis Enterprise*, I stated that ECR would not deliver results because it did not go beyond EDI/AutoID/WMS to establish true partnerships. This has now been proven true.

In a similar way, if supply chains today address only of one of the eight core competencies of SCS, they will not succeed. All eight must be pursued. So, B2B is important, but unto itself, it will not deliver the supply chain results needed to achieve the synthesis of the supply chain, the chain with No Boundaries that will result in true competitive advantage in today's supply chain marketplace battles.

It is time for companies to move beyond the siloism of SCM and embrace the total integration process of Supply Chain Synthesis. SCS will bring you and your supply chain increased Return on Assets (ROA), improved customer satisfaction, maximized speed, reduced costs, and the integration of the total supply chain. It will assure that your B2B communications translate to real results and that your chain will achieve competitive advantage over all competing chains.

This book will show you how you can pursue all eight SCS core competencies and achieve awesome supply chain results.

The supply chains you create with this book will exist with No Boundaries and will result in tremendous competitive advantage. So, SCS is a bold new journey—but it is the only way to travel for your organization and for your chain to win in today's global marketplace. It is time to begin the journey.

BEYOND SUPPLY CHAIN MANAGEMENT

"When there are no limits to whom you see, where you'll go, what you'll touch, the results are remarkable."

—Jack Welch, CEO, GE

Industry is looking for an answer. What is the question? Simply, it is "How do we keep our customers happy, grow our business, and increase profitability?"

The answer to this question has been "Supply Chain Management." For 15 years, Supply Chain Management (SCM) has tried to be the panacea for poor customer service, poor communication, and poor relationships. Yet, despite all of our SCM efforts, we are still losing ground. This is not due to neglect of the supply chain. Organizations know well the importance of the supply chain: According to a 1998 Deloitte and Touche survey, 90 percent of the companies surveyed planned supply chain improvements in 1999, but only 2 percent believed their supply chain used best practices.

The supply chain is important; that has not changed. However, I believe that, due to our lack of success with SCM, it is now time to move beyond SCM. The fact is that SCM has lacked scientific underpinning. SCM is about optimizing individual links, and this is no longer sufficient. Competition today is not about my link versus your link; the competition today is my chain versus your chain and a link optimization approach is now inadequate.

To deliver maximum value, customization, and satisfaction to the ultimate customer, while at the same time reducing inventory, trimming lead times, and reducing costs, the supply chain must become one entity, with No Boundaries, the goal of which is to satisfy the ultimate customer. To become one entity, the supply chain must be synthesized. The result is Supply Chain Synthesis (SCS).

WHAT IS SUPPLY CHAIN SYNTHESIS?

SCS is a holistic, continuous improvement process of ensuring customer satisfaction from the original raw material provider to the ultimate, finished-product consumer. In other words, it is doing business with No Boundaries. It is holistic because it is concerned with a complete chain, rather than one link. It is a continuous improvement process that is infinite; it never stops. SCS melts the links in the supply chain into a smooth continuous flow. Visualize a river, properly banked and channeled, that is flowing toward a goal and you are also visualizing SCS. A river has no links, and although thousands of separate, natural forces comprise it, it is seen as one entity.

FROM CHAIN TO RIVER

"Without banks the river is just a puddle."
                    —Mark Twain

A river must have banks, or as Mark Twain says, it will be a puddle. The SCS riverbanks are Integration and Change. Without one or the other or both, SCS is nothing but a puddle, with no force or destination. The breadth of Integration and the rate of Change are creating movement and force, yet there seems to be a lack of understanding of the effect each has on SCS. If you gain a solid understanding of Integration and Change, then it will provide you with a set of requirements in tomorrow's business climate.

In the 1980s, integrating within processes was the Integration focus. Then, in the 1990s, the opportunity to integrate between processes became apparent, and with this new Integration focus, SCM was born. The thrust was to integrate manufacturing and distribution to create an integrated supply chain via SCM. SCM was viewed as the ultimate Integration, and many companies and business gurus still agree. It is easy to understand why: Integration may be viewed at different levels, depending on the vantage point. If you are hovering six feet above the ground in a hot air balloon, then the worker in the workstation looks like Integration. As your balloon goes up, you see Integration as man/workstation/equipment, then as material handling systems, then as manufacturing systems, and then as SCM. You are now a mile above the ground, and your balloonist may tell you there is no need to go any higher or that there are greater risks at a higher point. But if you insist and he complies, then you reach the vantage point where Integration is at its highest level: SCS.

So, from an Integration perspective, we see that there is a progressively expanding concept of what SCS means and how it functions. A company's leadership must ride that balloon as high as it can go to have the broadest perspective and ensure its success. Part of that larger view includes the second riverbank—Change.

There are two primary drivers of change. They are people and technology. Take some time to think about these facts:

1. In 1860, one billion people populated the planet. In 1999, that number reached six billion.
2. Eighty percent of technological advances have occurred since 1900.
3. Available information doubles every five years.

SAY THAT AGAIN?

There are a few quotes I want to share with you as we think about Change:

- In 1876, Western Union, after an in-depth study, said, "The telephone has too many shortcomings to be seriously considered as a means of communication."
- Harry Warner, one of the Warner Brothers, said, "Who the hell wants to hear actors talk?"
- Early in the computer era, Ken Olson, the founder, President, and CEO of Digital Equipment and also the man who created one of the most successful computer companies in the country said, "There is no reason for any individual to have a computer in the home."

Isn't it interesting to see what happens when we don't keep Change in view? As business leaders, we must, with obsession, remember that we are in the 🖋 portion of the graph, lest we make an ill-informed decision about our industry and miss the boat.

Here are a few more quotes that apply to living in the 🖋.

- Glasgow said, "The trouble with the future is that it usually arrives before we are ready for it."
- Ashleigh Brilliant said, "Strangely enough, this is the past that somebody in the future is longing to go back to."
- Lily Tomlin said, "We're all in this alone."

People are driving Change because there are so many of us now. We went from one billion people in 1860, to two billion in 1935, to four billion in 1975, to six million in 1999. Not only is the world growing, but it also is growing at an increasingly rapid rate. If we graph the "people" variables (length of life, income, transport speed, population) in the history of Change, there is a flat line, then a slight curve, and then a sharp curve (𝒮). Today we are living in the 𝒮 .

This ever-expanding population is living longer and becoming more demanding. In the days before automobiles, if a family that wanted to take a trip on a stagecoach was told, "Sorry, but the last stagecoach has already left. You've got to wait a week," they'd say, "No problem. It's only a week." Now, if we miss a section in a revolving door, we get upset. If we are caught by a red light, we start banging on the steering wheel and yelling, "I've got to go."

Few people drive the speed limit anymore. The time it takes for us to log onto our e-mail server seems to be forever, and we complain about how slow it is, when, in reality, it only takes about eight seconds.

In the U.S., another change being driven by people is where we work. For example, in 1900, 85 percent of the population worked in agriculture, 10 percent in production, and 5 percent in service. Today, about 1 percent of the U.S. population works on the farm, 13 percent works in production, and 86 percent works in service. Yet, we are producing more wealth in agriculture— $200 billion in annual sales—today than we have ever produced in the history of our country. In manufacturing, we produce 23 percent of our gross domestic product in the factory. We are as strong in manufacturing as we have been any time since the statistics were first kept in 1947. We have an agricultural-manufacturing based economy, not a service economy. Sure, more people work in the service sector, and productivity and yield in agriculture and manufacturing have grown to the point of not needing a lot of people, but of the 86 percent of the population that are in the service sector, many service the agricultural and manufacturing sectors. So, the biggest change is not where people work, but that wealth generation is no longer based on resources, but rather on knowledge. The world's economy is no longer driven by capital; instead it is driven by knowledge.

Like the population, technology is driving Change because it is exploding. The most dramatic explosion in technology is the

Internet. Business transactions on the Internet are increasing exponentially. Amazing predictions are being made:

1. More than half of America's mainstream companies will be selling their products and services online by the end of the year 2000.
2. By the year 2000, over 200 million users will be connected to the Internet.
3. By the year 2002, Internet commerce in the U.S. will generate revenue of over $1.1 trillion.
4. The Internet doubles in traffic every 100 days; nothing else in the world, other than bacteria, grows that fast.

THE ✍ OF TECHNOLOGY

As Lew Pritchett, formerly of Procter & Gamble stated: "Success in the next century will depend on access to information, not access to capital." But how we shift culturally toward information attainment and utilization is a major issue. This may be most prevalent in the following observations:

- Web-based training is embraced by many companies—even though half of the respondents in a recent EDS survey said they like traditional classroom training better.
- The worldwide smart card industry is projected to reach $2.2 billion in revenue within the next few years—if the industry agrees on standards and depth of marketing efforts.
- XML may eliminate EDI—if the industry agrees on standards and protocols for the data-driven mark-up language.

What is most amazing about these statements is that they may err on the side of caution. The Internet and e-business are growing and moving so quickly that it is difficult to predict the future.

I read a *Putman Investment* ad that said, "You think you understand the situation, but what you don't understand is that the situation just changed." As soon as you know something, everything changes. In 1900, it was predicted that by 1919, everyone in America would be working in the fields and there would be a land shortage. These seers missed the point on two issues: productivity and yield. As productivity and yield have grown, not only is there enough food for everyone to eat, but there is enough to export. By the 1950s, many agricultural workers had left the farm and gone to the factory. So then the seers predicted that by 1970, everyone would be in the factory producing goods. They believed that, as the standard of living improved, people would try to acquire more things, thereby creating a need for more workers to produce them. These seers had learned nothing from the agriculture revolution and once again, they did not take Change into account. Now, as we start a new century, we see that the number of people required to produce all those things they were imagining in the 1950s is 13 percent of the population.

Seers who believed they had a handle on the Internet revolution have already begun to miss the boat when addressing the impact it is having on business. Many pundits believed that e-business would be "incredibly efficient clusters of computer programmers who used subcontractors to handle such dreary tasks as keeping inventory, filling orders, and handling customer service issues." These pundits discounted people in their prophecy. The Internet, because it connects people and information quicker, easier, and at minimal cost, allows people to make better decisions. Buyers can easily compare products, prices, and services, as well as communicate with far more people than they have in the past. New relationships are forged daily, and, when they are vendor-customer relationships, the playing field is leveled, reducing the value of branding and accelerating margin pressures. The importance of providing quality service and high levels of customer satisfaction becomes paramount.

Like all seers, past and present, if you attempt to look at anything without understanding the impact of Change, you will fall on your face. Your business will not work. Yet, many are doing exactly that with SCM. SCM focuses on the optimization of a static environment. SCS understands that the only way to handle Change and the dynamic environment that is the result of Change is by using a continuous improvement process that addresses changing requirements as they occur.

MANAGEMENT BY FAD

Many people think that approaches are the way to harness Change. It is much easier to grasp an approach than it is to understand and implement a process. An approach focus, rather than a process focus, creates what I call Management By Fad (MBF). When what they are doing isn't working, people often reach out and grab first one thing and then another. First they do it, then they re-do it, then they are beyond re-doing it. They engineer, reengineer, re-reengineer, and then they are beyond engineering. They try on a new technique and insist that it fits until the seams finally burst. They then go in search of the next style and size. Many wait for an expert to arrive and explain the next technique so that they may print a slogan on a coffee mug and feel better.

Today's challenges cannot be resolved by shellacking a layer of fad over them. We must ride that balloon to the highest level and look at the panorama that it creates, using our framework of Integration and Change. SCS will power us to that level and let us see not just today's challenges, but challenges that we can't even imagine at this point.

WHERE DO WE GO FROM HERE?

The vision of the future requires us to move beyond the SCM approach. Before that happens, we must take a hard look at SCM to see how this approach may be used as a building block for a process—the SCS process. SCM is truly a logistical concept. It is not something you view from a Total Operations point of view. SCS is a Total Operations point of view and therefore, to do it well, we must do not only logistics, but also manufacturing, maintenance, quality, and organizational excellence. That is why

SCM has a place in SCS, but it is not SCS and never will be.

This book presents, in detail, how SCS works, how it can enable your organization to reach unparalleled levels of performance, and how any organization can use the eight core competencies required to synthesize its supply chain.

2

WHAT'S GOING ON TODAY?

"All change is a miracle to contemplate; but it is a miracle which is taking place every second."

—Henry David Thoreau

So much is happening. The 🖎 we discussed in Chapter 1 is changing the way we view business. We are also being presented with various challenges. SKUs continue to grow, boundaries between manufacturing and distribution are blurring, and deverticalization—a de-layering activity that creates the opposite of a vertical industry—is becoming a trend. These have also brought about what I consider the major challenges of Change: Channel Structure and Relationships, Customer Satisfaction, Information Systems and Technology, and a Global Economy. All of these challenges must be viewed through the filters of Integration and Change.

CHANNEL STRUCTURE AND RELATIONSHIPS

In today's business climate, channel structures are blurring and relationships are fluid. Industry is removing links from the supply chain, and alternate channels such as catalogs and the Internet are growing tremendously. Not only will that growth rate continue, but it will also increase.

Consider the electronics industry. Retailers view computers as a perishable commodity because they have a short shelf life. Retailers who missed this key point are now suffering the consequences of overstocks on "expired" computers.

When channel structures and relationships change, de-layering, outsourcing, and deverticalization become reality. The impact these strategies have is unbelievable. Sometimes they add links to the supply chain, and sometimes they remove links. Whether they add or subtract links, they have major implications on how businesses are organized. For example, the electronics industry is seeing a surge in growth of contract electronic manufacturers (CEMs). Today's CEMs are offering more manufacturing, design, and logistics services to OEMs. According to a *Purchasing* magazine survey, 47 percent of all electronics manufacturing for original equipment manufacturers (OEMs) is outsourced, and 54 percent of computer, peripheral, communications, automotive, medical, and industrial control OEMs look to CEMs for manufacturing solutions. OEMs rely on CEMs to reduce their manufacturing costs, lower inventory, and avoid purchasing or leasing capital equipment. Savings in manufacturing average 26 percent. This has proven so attractive that one-third of those surveyed expect to use CEMs more in the next year, and according to a February 2000 *Fortune* article, "The term OEM, in fact, has become dated; today these companies could more accurately be called OBHs (original brand holders)."

Information technology (IT) is also developing outsourcing relationships. There has been a proliferation of application service providers (ASPs), third-party entities that manage and distribute software-based services and solutions to customers across a wide area network from a central data center. In other words, ASPs allow companies to outsource some or all of their IT needs. Many are commercial, but some are government and/or nonprofit organizations.

THE VALUE OF OUTSOURCING—SOLECTRON

Solectron, one of the largest contract manufacturers in the world, was cited as the No. 3 organization in the 1999 *Business Week* Info Tech 100. Its global presence includes representation in 21 countries. Solectron's dominance in the contract manufacturer (CM) market can be traced to several factors:

- Its efficiency
- Its ability to exploit its high volume
- Its willingness to provide value-added services to original equipment manufacturers (OEMs).

As for efficiency, Solectron spends almost nothing on frills, and its overhead is 4 percent of sales. By virtue of its diverse and large customer base, the company can leverage itself against vendors to receive discounts on materials, and Solectron passes these discounts on to the OEM. Solectron also derives more use out of each piece of equipment as a result of its order volume. Finally, this CEM enables its OEMs to concentrate on high-level design and brand recognition by taking on the less glamorous aspects of manufacturing and repair, as well as logistics and purchasing.

The partnerships that corporations establish represent a leap over one of the highest hurdles in American business: the "us versus them" mentality of supplier/customer relationships. Recent trends in commerce, such as supplier certification, provide added value to the end product and strengthen the supply chain as a result. Ultimately, those who truly understand and practice partnerships will triumph as channel structures and relationships change.

THE VALUE OF PARTNERING—FURNITURE.COM

The U.S. furniture industry, with an estimated value of $178 billion, is notorious for being manufacturing-driven with slow cycle times. Furniture.com decided to do something about this.

Says Carl Prindle, executive producer at Furniture.com, "Putting the customer at the center isn't something that this industry usually does. There are so many frustrations: the length of time that you have to wait, the fact that you may have to go to five or six stores to find the style you want."

Prindle and Furniture.com CEO Andrew Brooks have reinvented the furniture-buying experience and moved it to the Web. Their main focus is to change the notion of a 6- to 12-week period between an order for furniture and its delivery. It has gathered information about its customers' preferences and shared that data with its partners: several North Carolina furniture manufacturers. These manufacturers then produce a limited set of furniture pieces based on that information and that allows them to meet the three-week delivery time Furniture.com requires.

"In the world of e-commerce, three weeks is an eternity," says Brooks. "But in the world of furniture, it's a snap of the fingers. Our vision is to collaborate with customers and manufacturers to make this a better experience. This is an industry that has a lot of room for improvement."

—*Net Company*, Fall 1999

CUSTOMER SATISFACTION

Customization, *customer choice*, *customer control*, *customer relationship management*, and *customer-centric* are increasingly being used to describe manufacturing focus, a change from the enterprise-wide focus that once characterized manufacturing just a few years ago. As Janet Gould, in her article in the June 1999 issue of *IDS*, wrote, "The 'good old days'—when Henry Ford dictated that the customer could have his Model T in any color as long as it was black—are history." Basically, customer needs and desires are dictating what manufacturers produce—and any manufacturer that does not listen will be left behind. And if customers are now dictating what is being produced, then customer satisfaction becomes paramount.

Part of the challenge of customer satisfaction for many companies is understanding that it is not the same as traditional customer service. The basic formula for customer satisfaction is:

Customer Satisfaction = Customer Perception of the Service Received – Customer Expectation of Customer Service.

The customer satisfaction formula presupposes two critical statements that every organization seeking to revolutionize customer satisfaction must assimilate:

1. Customer satisfaction is based on our customers' perceptions and expectations, not on our self-centered view of what the customer may want.
2. The level of customer satisfaction will change as customers' expectations change.

Customer satisfaction requires us to divest our self-interest and to focus on the needs, expectations, and perceptions of those to whom we provide products and services. Because customers change while they are our customers, companies cannot maintain customer satisfaction with the same set of services and value-adds that satisfied the customer yesterday. As customers progress in their patronage, they expect more and require more to be satisfied. For our customer satisfaction to be high, we must separate our customers into categories or tiers. These tiers—visitors, associates, and partners—should then be treated in a way that reflects the profit they are bringing to us.

This separation helps us enjoy customers that are highly satisfied while maximizing our profit. With so many new demands, like the SKU explosion and increased product customization, being placed on companies every day, the ability to keep customer satisfaction levels high will be critical. This will especially be true as these two trends continue their rapid growth in the years to come.

How will you be able to keep up while significantly improving customer satisfaction? SCS can answer that question. By synthesizing all the links in the chain and creating a river, you will be able to know your customers, serve your customers, and satisfy your customers. You will develop new practices that can identify individual customer needs and expectations and meet them with products and services that represent unique value for each customer. The flow of communication in the SCS environment will allow trimmed lead times, cost reductions, and quality improvements. The creativity of the entire supply chain will be brought to bear on the ultimate customer's needs.

INFORMATION SYSTEMS AND TECHNOLOGY

Many of us reminisce about the days before voice mail and e-mail, LANs, WANs, and VANs, intranets and extranets, video conferencing and whiteboarding, streaming and webcasts. Technology can make us crazy, but it is undoubtedly a driving force in bringing our world closer. Applied correctly, it brings out the best in our people, and harnesses creativity in team and individual environments.

Here are a few recent headlines:

- "The Internet Opportunity—And More"
- "Computational Fluid Dynamics for Design Optimization"
- "E-mail Manages Work Documents"
- "Making Information Part of the Package"

IT is moving forward faster than we can imagine. The Internet is connecting people and information quicker, easier, and at a minimal cost. The World Wide Web has evolved from a place for brochureware to a place for dialogue and relationships. This levels the playing field among competitors and accelerates margin pressures, reduces the value of branding, and increases the importance of providing quality service.

Off the Web, Auto ID, communications technology, and business software are being standardized and systems integrators are writing custom interfaces to allow the exchange of data between various applications. Also, middleware is developing rapidly, creating ways to tie disparate programs and systems together through enterprise application integrators (EAI) and web application servers.

SCS exploits information systems, the Internet, and technology to create electronic SCS (e-SCS). With e-SCS, companies can extend their market reach and accomplish things beyond the scope of current imagination. As Paul Allen, Microsoft's "other" founding father, says, "Current implemented technology represents only 10 percent of the existing cache." Imagine what the world will look like when even 90 percent is implemented. It is beyond the ✍.

GLOBAL ECONOMY

The success of firms depends heavily now on their ability to reach foreign markets. Business no longer ends at the border of a particular country or continent. "No Boundaries" is more than a phrase. Two factors have affected this new global economy: politics and technology. Politically, the last two decades have eliminated some of the isolationism that has plagued business. Trade agreements have been established to ease the tensions and reticence between once-competing nations. Major trade agreements made in the last two decades include

- North American Free Trade Agreement (NAFTA)— between Canada, the United States, and Mexico
- South American Common Market (Mercosur)—between Argentina, Brazil, Paraguay, and Uruguay
- Andean Pact—between Bolivia, Colombia, Ecuador, Peru, and Venezuela
- Central American Common Market—between Costa Rica, El Salvador, Guatemala, Honduras, and Nicaragua
- European Union (EU)—formation of a single economic market in Europe integrated further by the recent introduction of the Euro, a currency to be shared by most of its members.

Technology also plays a role in this global economy. The Internet has made the world smaller, and, in fact, has made geography irrelevant. With the speed of information delivery and the shrinking distances that it creates between markets, the supply chains we are competing against may be halfway around the world rather than across town. In many cases, when we are using the Internet to disseminate information, we may not even know its destination.

New trade agreements, individual countries partnering with each other to produce and export goods, international e-commerce, and web applications are only a few of the many challenges presented by the global marketplace. Their numbers will continue to increase. To address them robustly, we must use SCS.

THE MYTHS OF THE PAST

The unbelievable rate of Change affects everything that takes place. At the time that we accept this concept, we must also put a myth behind us: In business, the past is not a good indicator of the future. Nowhere is this more evident than in our fast-paced, merger-and-acquisition world. A client that, two months ago, was two completely different companies is at present one company with a combination of 44 distribution centers. If this company relies on its past to predict its future, it will go out of business.

We should not ignore the past. Instead, we should understand that the future is an extension of the present based upon the background of the past. The future is not an extension of the past, and if we are to meet today's challenges, create a vision of the future, and achieve SCS, we must remember that.

3

A FOUNDATION
FOR THE FUTURE

"There will be two types of companies in the future. The quick
and the dead."

—Charles Wang, Chairman,
Computer Associates International

People are always trying to forecast the future. Many base
their forecasts on the past. This is a mistake that can catch
us all. It happens because, at one time, using the past to
develop forecasts worked. However, due to the present rate of
Change, using the past to develop forecasts no longer works. If
we examine the word "forecast" carefully, we can see how
forecasting is bound to fail. The word "fore" is from golf, and it
means "duck!" The word "cast" is from fishing, and it means to
"throw out." If we are alternately ducking and throwing out, we
are reacting and not predicting. In most cases, we are reacting to
the past and then using it to predict the future. Today's rate of
Change has created a permanent whitewater that demands an

understanding of the present and the impact it will have on the future.

Because Integration and Change are the riverbanks of this whitewater, the SCS foundation for the future allows us to grasp them both. The foundation is divided neatly in half, with six parts that are a result of grasping Integration (total integration, blurred boundaries, consolidation, reliability, maintainability, and economic progressiveness) and six parts that are the requirements for harnessing Change (flexibility, modularity, upgradeability, adaptability, selective operability, and automation supportability). These elements are all relevant to where we are headed and a significant understanding of these concepts, along with the impact of e-business, results in a foundation upon which an understanding of SCS may be based.

TOTAL INTEGRATION

Total integration is an ultimate focus where material flow is designed from the top of the SCS perspective. In other words, it is the Integration of material and information flow in a true, top-down progression that begins with the customer. For example, a company that makes fiber, another company that makes fabric, yet another that dyes fabric, and one that makes dresses should all be thinking of the person planning to buy a dress.

When the ultimate customer is not the focus, then the end result could be like that of the fiber manufacturer that asked Tompkins to study their supply chain and help them understand it. When asked why they wanted a study of the supply chain, they said that a special fiber that had done really well in the early market produced a dress that was returned by customers after the purchase. The fiber manufacturer, the fabric maker, the dye house, the dress house, and the retailer all lost money. A Tompkins Associates analysis showed that the dress was returned because it had static cling. Had all these companies focused on the fact that customers don't like static cling and planned accordingly, this story might have had a different conclusion.

Total integration is both broad and holistic. Individual relationships are not part of this perspective because customer satisfaction is only achieved from a synthesis of the whole supply chain. Therefore, business systems are integrated. Products are not being delayed on the dock because no one knows what is in the container. No one is re-entering information that has already been entered by the shipping company. Instead, automatically received advance shipping notices (ASNs) are being used, cross-docking is being considered, and inventory is being discussed with vendor management. There are no surprises because SCS is truly focused on the integration of the process for the total good: the satisfaction of the ultimate customer. A foundation for the future with SCS, therefore, includes total integration.

THE VALUE OF TOTAL INTEGRATION—BROTHER INTERNATIONAL

Brother International manufactures printers, fax machines, and multifunction products. The design focus of its Bartlett, Tennessee, facility, which spans more area than 24 football fields, was total integration of Brother International's operations. To achieve this end, the facility was outfitted with an advanced barcode control system and a highly evolved IT system, automated conveyor systems for hands-off material handling and high-level energy management systems.

As a result of the changes, the number of orders shipped from the Bartlett plant has increased tremendously. For example, in 1994, 130,500 orders were shipped from the plant. A year later, it shipped about 191,500, which represents a 40 percent increase. That number rose to almost 395,000 in 1997, a 200 percent increase over the rate of a few years ago. In terms of labor productivity, shipments per worker were up about 165 percent during those years.

—*Purchasing*, March 25, 1999

BLURRED BOUNDARIES

By its very nature, Integration shifts traditional customer/supplier and manufacturing/warehousing boundaries in the processes of simplifying, adding value, and being responsive. In the SCS foundation for the future, where there is total integration, these boundaries are blurred to the point where there are No Boundaries. The relationships between order entry, service, manufacturing, distribution, and other facets of a company are less defined. This blurring of boundaries is not limited to within a company, but also applies to external relationships.

In a 1998 *Harvard Business Review* interview, Michael Dell said, "...you're basically stitching together a business with partners that are treated as if they are inside the company. You're sharing information in real-time." He described an example of traditional supplier communications as "Well, every two weeks deliver 5,000 to this warehouse, and we'll put them on the shelf, and then we'll take them off the shelf." He explained that Dell tells its suppliers the daily production requirements: "Tomorrow morning we need 8,562 [units] and deliver them to door number seven by 7 a.m." He then added, "You would deal with an internal supplier that way, and you can do so because you share information and plans very freely."

So, inside a company or out, siloism is no longer the answer. Silos were developed because they provide comfort, allowing us to say, "Well, I know my job. I am product director of this product; I am product manager on that. If I do these two things well, then I am going to be successful." Staying in a comfort zone with clearly defined boundaries is one of the quickest paths to failure. SCM will keep you in the comfort zone; SCS has No Boundaries. It will take you out of the comfort zone and lead you to customer satisfaction, increased growth, and increased profitability.

CONSOLIDATION

The word "consolidation" may bring to mind the client with 44 distribution centers that would like to reduce that number to two. However, that is only the tip of the iceberg. Industry consolidations are rising in number and speed. Financial institutions are merging globally, as are printing companies, publishing companies, telecommunications companies, and pharmaceutical companies. The results are fewer and stronger competitors, customers, and suppliers, as well as consolidation layers such as site consolidations, company consolidations, and functional consolidations, all of which may take place at the same time.

The SCS foundation for the future capitalizes on consolidations. During mergers and acquisitions, consolidation often is a natural result of an action. One company buys another and then eliminates clearly duplicated functions or sites. Consolidation, however, may also be the result of great effort and persistence. Efficient and effective transportation infrastructures and economies of scale that provide for higher throughput levels and customization also create consolidation. Redundancies become merely remnants or memories of the past. What allows these efficient, effective infrastructures, these higher throughput levels, and this customization? SCS.

RELIABILITY

Robust systems, redundant systems, and fault-tolerant systems demand complete reliability, as do streamlined requirements, increased response time, and total inter-relatedness. The high levels of uptime these factors create makes reliability even more critical. Inventory can no longer substitute for the downtime caused by unreliable processes.

In turn, reliability can also cut production times and reduce failure rates. For example, an x-ray film processing manufacturer wanted to decrease the processor assembly time. The reliability of the connectors they chose for the manufacturing process eventually resulted in an assembly time of 1.5 hours instead of six. The failure rate decreased 28 percent.

MAINTENANCE

To achieve the continuous reliability requirements that the future will demand, 24/7 maintenance is also critical, even though there will be less time and fewer people to maintain equipment.

Therefore, preventive maintenance and predictive maintenance will be key. Preventive maintenance is a continuous process, the objective of which is to minimize future maintenance problems. Predictive maintenance anticipates potential problems by sensing the operations of a machine or system and must be used to perform system self-assessment and maintenance scheduling. SCS realizes that preventive and predictive maintenance are not only the highest levels of maintenance but are key Integration requirements.

THE VALUE OF ECONOMIC PROGRESSIVENESS—PROCTER & GAMBLE

"Restructuring" and "retooling" were the keynotes in CEO Durk Jager's address to business analysts in June 1999. Procter & Gamble, the titan of consumer goods, was facing a crossroads: Take the safe path and realize minimal growth, or embrace change by taking the unknown path. Jager plans to take the risk.

P & G will slash annual costs by $900 million through a mixture of layoffs and plant closings. This vision represents a dynamic shift in the culture of the company based in Cincinnati, Ohio, where employees have traditionally worked quietly to retirement and never rocked the boat.

The company is facing monumental obstacles that are preventing it from truly breaking into global markets: lengthy research and development, reinvention of products for international marketing, and reliance on outmoded marketing strategies (e.g., advertising during daytime television). One of Jager's projects—to test a new mop in French and U.S. markets simultaneously—reduced the time for global introduction from five years to 18 months.

With new target markets and a more global approach to its product lines, P & G is hoping to become a responsive organization for the 21st century.

ECONOMIC PROGRESSIVENESS

In the SCS foundation for the future, progressive, forward-thinking decisions must be based upon the SCS perspective and not the economic justification of the individual link, plant, or department. Again, we'll look at this from Michael Dell's perspective. In the *Harvard Business Review* interview, he said, "Until you look inside and understand what's going on by business, by customer, by geography, you don't know anything." And he is absolutely right.

Evolution, growth, and Change are constantly taking place; therefore, all decisions we make must be based on a very broad view of the future. We need to adopt innovative practices that integrate scattered information into a whole that can be used for decision making, such as deploying customer-direct strategies over the World Wide Web or exploiting the Internet to improve agility and produce cost savings. Any individual solution must be based on where we as a whole are going next; we cannot focus on a solution that is only for the here and now. Economics must be viewed progressively so that we can adapt over time.

FLEXIBILITY AND MODULARITY

Flexibility and modularity are the first of the six requirements necessary for Change in the SCS foundation for the future. Build-to-order (BTO) manufacturing is growing rapidly. It seems everyone is jumping on the BTO bandwagon, from PC makers, to automakers, to seismic-enclosure makers. No longer does it make sense to build to stock and then configure the order. Instead, companies are receiving the order and then building the stock, and the only way to keep up with the demand is through flexibility and modularity.

Although flexibility and modularity are both necessary in the total integration and BTO environments, there is a difference between the two. Flexibility means being able to handle a variety of requirements without being altered. Flexible manufacturing systems, therefore, are those able to produce a variety of different products without altering the manufacturing operation. These systems must be "soft" and "friendly" rather than "hard" and "rigid" because they must be able to address the Change in variety and handle products that vary in size and features.

Whereas flexibility deals with variety, modularity deals with volume. Modular manufacturing operations are those that can produce more or less of a product without changing the method. Products made to order must be made quickly when the orders are received, so systems must cooperate efficiently over a wide range of operating rates.

Manufacturing has changed and will continue to change. With flexible and modular manufacturing processes, supply chain partners can address Change, and achieve SCS.

THE VALUE OF FLEXIBILITY AND MODULARITY—COACH

Coach, which is headquartered in Manhattan, New York, is a manufacturer of luxury leather goods and has been a division of the Sara Lee Corporation since 1985. Coach employs more than 4,000 people in 15 countries, and distributes its products globally. Coach uses various distribution channels including department stores, a mail order catalog, 150 Coach-owned retail outlets, and an International Division, to compete in the upper tier of the leather goods market.

In 1993, the Coach's Carlstadt, New Jersey, factory began a conversion from a batch manufacturing facility to a quick-response factory. The Carlstadt factory used various manufacturing practices (e.g. Toyota Production System practices) to reduce setup time during style changeovers and create the flexibility necessary for meeting dramatic increases in customer demand and expanding style offerings. As a result, each of its production modules has now become a mini-factory that can produce all the leather goods offered by Coach.

—*Modern Materials Handling*, August 1, 1999

UPGRADEABILITY

The changing manufacturing environment, from "if we build it, they will come" to "they have come, so we must build," also demands that systems and processes be upgradeable. Upgradeability is the ability, with a minimum amount of downtime, to gracefully incorporate advances in equipment, systems, and technology. All sorts of products, from computer drives to battery re-chargers to dc converters are now featuring upgradeability. With the accelerated rate of Change, it is not nor will it be economical to replace entire systems as we have in the past. Instead, the system should be able to move to the next level without stumbling or hiccuping and with little downtime. Therefore, upgradeability is inherent in SCS.

ADAPTABILITY

The fourth requirement of Change, adaptability, provides a setting for flexibility, modularity, and upgradeability. We may have a beautiful strategic master plan, thinking we know everything will work. We use the process of SCS and everything seems perfect and on target. But what happens if a portion goes wrong or an external factor changes?

An adaptive environment allows us to take sudden changes in stride. Traditionally, emphasis has been placed on the control of operations to conform to system requirements at a "steady-state" level. Steady state no longer exists and averages are irrelevant. Systems now must be adaptive to respond to future system requirements.

Adaptability takes into consideration the implications of schedules, calendars, cycles, and peaks. It allows a system to work well at 9:15 a.m. on a Tuesday in the summer slow season and work well at 2:30 p.m. on a Friday during peak demand times. The design, from an operations perspective, must allow it to work for a one-hour time frame, a two-hour time frame, or a two-week time frame. Adaptability also recognizes that product demand in various industries is higher at some time than others and can adjust accordingly. If you build adaptability into your plans, processes, and systems, you will rarely be caught by surprise. Instead, you will harness the energy of Change and achieve SCS.

SELECTIVE OPERABILITY

The ability to operate selectively is key to a successful SCS environment. Therefore, SCS elements must be able to operate in segments, allowing for implementation one segment at a time without degradation of the overall SCS system. SCS also requires understanding of how each segment operates. Then, if something goes wrong, we can answer questions such as "How did this take place? What has this done to our level of customer satisfaction?"

Selective operability also allows us to put contingency plans in place. A company that locates its distribution center on the North Carolina coast must plan for hurricanes so that other sites are not affected when a power outage, flooding, or roof damage occurs. If the company has a site in Wisconsin, it must be prepared for blizzards so that they do not affect production in a West Coast manufacturing plant. This can be tricky because operating in segments implies the individual links inherent in SCM, but in reality, it is not because it continues to view the chain as a whole entity. It is only by looking at the flow from start to finish that you can make contingency plans so that the flow does not come to a grinding halt in the middle.

AUTOMATION SUPPORTABILITY

The future promises more and more automation. Supply chain elements that are not automated now soon will be. Implementation will be piecemeal, and non-automated elements must support this type of implementation. Therefore, it is imperative that all elements throughout the synthesized supply chain not only support neighboring elements, but also integrate and interface with them. Integration is necessary for two automated processes, and interfacing is necessary for one process that is automated and one that is not.

THE FUTURE IS NOW: E-SCS

"In five years, you will either be in the e-business world, or you'll be out of business."

—Michael Capellas, CEO, Compaq

The SCS foundation for the future is not complete without "e-" because e- is affecting all elements of the supply chain. e- is being attached to commerce, procurement, marketplace, and business to signify the moving of supply chain processes to the Internet. e- is also a byproduct of Change and must be part of Integration.

Many firms have left verticality behind to become virtual enterprises. A virtual enterprise is one wherein enterprise activities are performed externally and not internally. The Internet is making more and more virtual enterprises a reality, and these enterprises are relying on e-business to handle their activities.

SCS understands e-. In fact, companies moving their supply chains to the Internet are practicing e-Supply Chain Synthesis: They are replacing traditional supply chain interactions with Web-based interactions. This has been a trend that has been growing for several years, but recent announcements that such big companies as Ford and GM are making their supply chains available on the World Wide Web in the first part of 2000, indicate that e-business will be the norm.

e-SCS does not differ from SCS. It is an extension of SCS. The following ten principles of e-SCS explain this extension:

1. e-SCS demands nimbleness. The e- and SCS revolution demands responsiveness as various e- and SCS opportunities present themselves. Scalability and flexibility must be built into all decisions because the revolutions not only will continue, they will continue at an ever-increasing pace.
2. e-SCS demands speed. All SCS activities must take place at the speed of e-. Any activity that functions at a rate slower than e- must be addressed because this will be a weak link in the overall supply chain.

3. e-SCS demands continuous improvement. With the pace of Change and the rate of innovation, what is a great strategy today will be suspect in a few months and obsolete shortly thereafter. All portions of the e-SCS strategy must be continually evaluated, analyzed, and improved.

4. e-SCS demands breadth. e-SCS must involve all aspects of the organization. No portion of the organization should be left as is; "business as usual" is no longer "business as usual."

5. e-SCS demands holism. The e-SCS strategy must go beyond the organization and include the entire supply chain. All e-SCS strategies must focus on the integrated pipeline.

6. e-SCS demands customer satisfaction. The e-SCS strategy must focus on the ultimate consumer and must not focus on the services provided by the supply chain, but rather the satisfaction derived by the customer.

7. e-SCS demands best practices. The requirements of the e-SCS business must be understood and then best practices installed to fulfill these requirements. As requirements evolve, so too must the best practices for fulfilling these new requirements.

8. e-SCS demands a global perspective. e- is global and thus e-SCS must be pursued from a global perspective. Regional approaches to SCS will be inappropriate be-cause e- cannot be regionalized or segmented. The only viable e-SCS strategies are global strategies.

9. e-SCS demands quality communications. Information delays or information silos will not be allowed. Emphasis must be placed on real-time sharing of information so that all supply chain links are responding to the same requirements.

10. e-SCS demands a focus on the bottom line. e-SCS must not lose sight of return on investments (ROI), return on assets (ROA), and profitability. Market share and share of mind are important startup strategies, but organizations must define in what time frame the e-efforts are expected

to begin achieving bottom-line results, and how much effort is needed to bring about these results.

To summarize, e-SCS requires nimbleness, speed, continuous improvement, breadth, holism, customer satisfaction, best practices, a global perspective, quality communications, and a focus on the bottom line. It has No Boundaries. These are all characteristics of SCS. However, e-SCS requirements emphasize speed a little more strongly than SCS, because the speed of e- demands it. Since all business is being impacted by e-, all business must move up to the speed of e-, and therefore, any activity that functions at a speed slower than e- must be addressed because otherwise it will become a weak link in the overall supply chain.

WHERE DO WE GO FROM HERE?

The SCS foundation for the future requires us to move beyond the SCM approach. To understand SCS, we must examine SCM to see why it isn't working and at the same time see how it can be used as a building block for the SCS process. Chapter 4 will discuss the problems of SCM and demonstrate why a process (SCS) must be substituted for an approach (SCM) for Total Operations success and Peak Performance.

4

Supply Chain Management Is Not Enough

"Is it sufficient that you have learned to drive the car, or shall we look and see what is under the hood?"
— June Singer, Psychologist, Jung Institute of Chicago

For years, there has been talk about the potential of SCM. What about the delivery? What do the facts say? Consider the following:

- The dry grocery supply chain in the U.S. now warehouses 106 days of inventory, when only a few years ago, it held 104 days.
- Last year, eight out of every 100 customers shopping for a specific item discovered that it was out of stock.
- Over the last four years in the U.S., there has been an ongoing loss in productivity and inventory levels are at an all-time high.
- Customer satisfaction fell again last year even though

organizations claim to be providing better and better customer service.

How can this be possible? How can companies practicing SCM have such high inventories? Why are customers not being satisfied? The answer is simple. The inventory levels are higher and customer satisfaction is lower because SCM is not enough.

From several important perspectives—trust, teamwork and partnerships, integration, and customer satisfaction—SCM is not the be-all and end-all approach to competitive advantage in the new millennium. In fact, some SCM initiatives have increased costs. The Manufacturing Assembly Pilot (MAP), a division of the Automotive Industry Action Group (AIAG) did a study that said that the automotive supply chain increased inefficiencies in the U.S. manufacturing sector to the tune of $1 billion a year. That translates into about $70 for each car produced in the U.S. in one year.

Why is SCM not enough? There are various reasons: omissions in the SCM model, the philosophy behind SCM, the fact that it is an approach and not a process, the issue of alliances, the growth of BTO, and the fact that SCM is a logistics concept. These reasons are discussed in this chapter.

FUNCTIONAL SILOS VS. TEAMWORK

A 1999 survey shows that, although companies are trying to encourage different departments to work together effectively, they continue to miss the mark in some cases. One of the reasons is that many of the professionals surveyed believe that cooperation and communication can allow different corporate functions to work together. However, they say using both tools is difficult because it is not the nature of corporations to promote them. In fact, some claim that unproductive habits, bad attitudes, and personal egos are preventing different departments from meshing.

The survey also reveals that many companies are not doing enough to foster cooperation between different departments and functions. Many survey respondents also claimed that their companies' efforts are actually counter-productive.

"There's too much competition among departments," says Ronald Blizzard, material administrator for Massachu-setts-based Guilford Rail System. His response was typical of many managers who say that long-standing rivalries between groups do not die easily or quickly.

Resistance to teamwork can be a result of the siloism inherent in SCM. Departments are viewing themselves as links that are attached to other departments and not as parts of a moving, flowing river.

OMISSIONS IN SCM

SCM does not address the issues of Integration and Change. It mentions both many times, but they truly are not part of the philosophy. How can it address either when it views the chain as a series of links rather than from a holistic point of view?

SCM also does not factor in transportation costs, link costs, customer satisfaction, improvement and quality, and manufacturing costs. One of the more unfathomable aspects of the model is in the Supply Chain Council's statement that manu-facturing costs are not affected by the Supply Chain. The blurred boundaries between distribution and manufacturing belie this statement. Since SCM omits manufacturing, that implies little or no concern for value adds and mass customization. Manufacturing must be part of the supply chain. There is no way around this, nor should there be.

So, the truth of the matter is that SCM is not complete. It omits Change, Integration, blurred boundaries, mass customization, manufacturing, and customer satisfaction. These are serious omissions and are among the many reasons why SCM is not working in today's environment.

THE SCM PHILOSOPHY

The philosophy behind SCM is "If I build it, the orders will
come." It can be broken down into three parts:

1. Supply—indicates a push
2. Chain—indicates individual, discrete links
3. Management—implies a static environment of control
   and measurement.

Problems are inherent in all three. "Push" no longer gets the
job done, because it gives control to suppliers rather than the
ultimate customer. Viewing the supply chain as individual links
is also problematic. Like the practice of medicine a century ago,
it treats symptoms but does not try to discover a cause. For
example, optimizing warehouse management without taking into
account other elements, such as sourcing and purchasing, production and inventory planning, transportation and distribution,
and customer satisfaction probably may not yield the desired
results. What may be creating warehousing problems may not
actually be a function of warehouse management, but something
else entirely. As for management, the static, controlled environment implied by the term also suggests containment. A healthy,
flowing supply chain is not contained; it cannot be for that would
make it resistant to Change.

The SCM philosophy, then, is one of push, links, and containment. Such a philosophy cannot succeed in a marketplace that
demands a combination of pull and push (not just push), flow
(not links), and harnessing (not managing) the energy of Change.
It does not supply the speed, flexibility, modularity, and unself-
ishness necessary in today's global and technological marketplace. It is no longer viable in this burgeoning build-to-order
(BTO), quick-response world—the world of No Boundaries.

NOT A PROCESS

What do Efficient Healthcare Response (EHCR), Efficient
Consumer Response (ECR), Efficient Foodstuff Response (EFR),
Quick Response (QR), Just-In-Time (JIT), Continuous Flow
Distribution, and SCM have in common? They are all approaches.
At one time, each has been viewed as the answer to high

inventory, high costs, and growing customer dissatisfaction. None has worked. Most have or will be discarded. Why? Again, because they are all approaches.

The problem with approaches is that they are not open-ended. Companies implement them once and expect results. They grasp at the approaches, but do not try to understand or maintain them for long periods of time. Today's challenges require processes, not approaches. Processes are open-ended. They shift, they change, they can be adjusted, and they *flow*. You can take a process at any point, review it, alter it, and improve it. You are not given that opportunity with approaches.

SCM is an approach that looks at a link with the aim of optimizing it. It does not robustly address change. It assumes that there is no marketplace turbulence and it also assumes that links may be optimized independently from the rate of Change. Any company that tries to optimize links while ignoring Change will face failure. Companies that rely on the SCM approach will face failure.

THE ISSUE OF ALLIANCES

SCM largely ignores alliances and partnerships. As a rule, executives do not see suppliers as partners. Recent surveys show that, for one reason or another, only 20 percent of North American and European executives see their suppliers as partners. This figure is higher than that of the Asia-Pacific rim (13 percent) and South America (8 percent). So, only 19 percent of executives worldwide see benefit in supplier partnerships. This is rooted in the traditional adversarial nature of purchaser/vendor relationships. It is also rooted in mistrust. In a May 20, 1999, article in *Purchasing* magazine, Anne Millen wrote what a lot of organizations are probably thinking: Close relationships, and their subsequent sharing of strategic information, lead to kickbacks, insider trading, and a sense of owning the vendor's time, product, and resources. This might be extreme, but the kernel of mistrust is there. SCM does not address these issues or assist companies in overcoming them. SCS does.

THE ISSUE OF BTO

SCM is not responsive to BTO. It is a push methodology, one that is built on the premise that products should be manufactured first and orders fulfilled second. BTO is a pull methodology where customer needs are considered first and then the products are manufactured.

How big is BTO? As Cisco Systems and Dell Computers find competitive advantage in their BTO philosophy, many other original equipment manufacturers (OEMs) are divesting themselves of the manufacturing operations altogether, paving the way for CEMs, both big niche players and smaller firms, to prosper. In 1997, according to a June 17, 1999 article in *Purchasing* magazine, about 24 percent, or $7.8 billion, of the top 50 contract manufacturers' sales come from BTO business. Eleven CEMs reported that 100 percent of their sales are for BTO. Nine CEMs say that BTO accounts for 50 to 99 percent of their business, and 17 reported that less than 50 percent of their business is BTO.

As BTO becomes the norm in some industries, such as electronics and computers, the supply chain must take up the call to arms. "There is a tidal wave of opportunity," says Michael Marks, the CEO of Flextronics. SCM does not allow companies to ride this wave. As Merrill Lynch has said, "The biggest shortfall in achieving Built-to-Order [success] is the lack of Supply Chain Management tools and methodology." Again, this is because SCM was not invented to adjust to such a big change in manufacturing methodology.

A LOGISTICS CONCEPT

SCM is a logistics concept. Logistics is defined as an organization's internal coordination of material management of raw material, material flow through production, and the physical distribution of finished goods. Logistics is within a link. Therefore, it is not surprising that SCM looks upstream and downstream, but only to improve the performance of the individual link. There is no continuous improvement of the whole supply chain, as SCM is not a supply chain concept, but a link and logistics concept.

THE VALUE OF E-COMMERCE FOR CEMS

OEMs are now using CEMs to lower manufacturing costs, so there is considerable pressure for the CEMs to reduce acquisition costs. EFTC, a Denver-based CEM, is lowering acquisition costs through e-commerce. EFTC developed JIT Net, a program that uses Electronic Data Interchange (EDI) to deliver forecasts every week to several distributors. Upon receipt of the forecasts, the distributors then ship parts to EFTC within two days. This arrangement has lowered inventory levels, cut procurement costs by about 20 precent, and reduced the number of purchasers needed because the purchasing process is automated.

EFTC has further plans for expanding its electronic interchanges. "We have room for improvement in inventory turns with more automation," says Bob Child, EFTC's director of corporate procurement. Currently, EFTC is on EDI with only a few suppliers. "There are more we could be doing it with," says Child. "EFTC uses JIT Net with several distributors for about 50 percent of the parts it buys. Now we need to extend it to printed circuit boards, transformers, and some custom, unique parts," says Child.

EFTC also is looking into web-based e-commerce solutions because they will provide the flexibility needed for build schedules. "We are getting shorter term forecasts from our customers than we used to and we are getting more requests for reschedules than we used to. That means we need more flexibility from our suppliers." He sees the Internet improving flexibility because information can be transmitted so efficiently and cheaply.

THE NEED IS CLEAR

Optimizing each link in the supply chain is no longer a sufficient practice. To deliver maximum value, customization, and satisfaction to the ultimate customer while at the same time reducing inventory, trimming lead times, and reducing costs, the supply chain must be integrated and synthesized to function as a single entity. The goal of this entity should be to satisfy the ultimate customer. No longer can the business mentality be "my company vs. your company." In today's marketplace, the thinking is "my supply chain vs. your supply chain." If a supply chain does not satisfy its ultimate customer, each link, one by one, will go out of business by default. This is a hard fact, but it is a reality. Keen business minds will see the opportunity in the challenge and readily shift their thinking to a total supply chain with No Boundaries so that they may individually and collectively prosper.

5

THE SUPPLY CHAIN SYNTHESIS OPPORTUNITY

"If you go slow, you will fall."
—Chris Stewart, Off-road Motorcycle Champion

Sometimes it amazes me just how much has taken place since we first developed the concept of SCS. It reminds me of my children. I was there when they were conceived, when they were born, and when they took their first steps, but I look at them now, and I am astonished at what I see. They have so many skills, capabilities, and opportunities; it is fantastic to me.

SCS is the same—and the pattern of its existence is the same. I was there when it was conceived, and I was there when it was born. At this point, what has occurred with SCS is almost unbelievable. The first step is to put this in some sort of context to catch up with where we are and where SCS is going. The second is to present the exciting opportunities of SCS.

HISTORICAL FRAMEWORK

Consider the history of technology: First there was the wheel, then the Industrial Revolution, electricity, the Machine Age, the fork truck, the conveyor, and the computer. Yet, none of these accomplishments gives us a framework within which we can discuss where we are today with respect to the supply chain. A better framework would be to consider the history of my growth; specifically, how I came to understand Integration and how the concept of SCS came to be.

BEYOND WORKER AND WORKPLACE

The first time I believe I understood the topic of Integration was in 1966. I was taking a course in work methods at Purdue University. I knew that integration was required between the worker and the workplace. Alone, the worker and workplace were individual elements. However, when someone combined them in an ergonomic way, the result was something special. I can recall very clearly my thought at the time, which was, "This is something I can grab onto. I now have an awareness of worker and workstation that I did not have before. This is exciting."

Then, in 1968, I worked as an intern under former President Nixon in Washington, DC. I worked on problems with the Post Office, and I began to understand that there was more to integration than worker and workplace. Conveyors were also involved. I soon realized their impact: changing the speed and changing the load being moved created an interaction that required an integrated, mechanical material handling equipment solution.

In the early 1970s, my thought processes changed once again. I focused on the worker, the workstation, material-handling equipment, and how the computer controlled the work environment. The integrated material-handling equipment grew into a material-handling system. Then I understood that there was more to it than just this system. I had to combine all the moves of the warehouse and the factory, and develop a system that handled the totality of distribution and the totality of manufacturing. So, in

1974, I wrote my first paper on material-handling systems and the importance of implementing them correctly.

In 1978, a client hired us to implement a material-handling system design in Texas. We designed the facility with automated guided vehicles, automated storage and retrieval, and state-of-the-art conveyor sortation. After the system was installed, I recall standing there on ribbon-cutting day and hearing how efficient the system was. But I thought, "This is not quality work." I realized then that what matters is not how well the material-handling system works, but what was important was how well the factory worked and how well the DC worked. It was not about material handling systems but manufacturing systems and distribution systems.

THE SUPPLY CHAIN

My realization at that ribbon-cutting ceremony changed my perspective until the early 1980s. When SCM came into being, I searched for the body of knowledge that would demonstrate its effectiveness. I could not find it. I decided that I could not find it because SCM was not a complete supply chain thought process. SCM looks upstream and downstream with the objective of optimizing individual links. I found that optimized links were not enough: I was interested in optimal chains. I also decided that optimization really was not the best word choice. "Optimization," by definition, indicates a predetermined objective function that must be maximized or minimized. We cannot optimize a supply chain today because of the rate at which the supply chain is evolving. What we should strive for is to have the best for that specific moment, but we must also focus on continuous improvement so that we continuously improve over time.

And that is where we are today. We need to synthesize the chain until there are No Boundaries. I view it like this: I see the big chain passing over the flame of synthesis, the flame melting the chain, and creating a flow of molten metal—SCS. The flow of SCS creates a world of opportunity for us.

THE SCS OPPORTUNITY

When he took on the task of redesigning his division's supply
chain, Dave Tronnes, Director of Manufacturing Administration
for the Toner Products Division of Toshiba realized he had to
address these supply chain trends:

1. Fewer supplies
2. Increased focus on customer satisfaction
3. Purchasers driving shorter cycle times
4. A greater role for design engineers on the sourcing team
5. Increased global sourcing
6. Increased single sourcing
7. Greater emphasis on strategic alliances with suppliers
8. Elimination of non-value-added supply chain activities
9. An increased role for purchasing professionals in strategic
   decision-making
10. Operational changes in the business process.

His goals included

- Lower purchase prices
- Lower transportation costs
- Reduced lead times on materials and supplies
- Higher quality supplies
- Increased profits and reduced (or unchanged) travel
- Increased communications capabilities through systems
  improvement.

How interesting. Tronnes has noticed the same trends I have.
His goals, based on these trends, are admirable. The opportuni-
ties presented to us by SCS are quite similar to Tronnes's goals.
Implementing SCS can

- Increase ROA
- Improve customer satisfaction
- Maximize speed
- Reduce costs
- Integrate the supply chain.

These are the opportunities of SCS. Let's take a closer look at
each.

INCREASE ROA

SCS increases ROA by maximizing inventory turns, minimizing obsolete inventory, maximizing employee participation, and maximizing continuous improvement. Traditionally, companies have tried to increase ROA by increasing the turns of the fast-moving products. But this nets minimal impact. Often the challenge is not the fast-moving product, but instead the slow-moving product. So, often the focus should not be on the most popular items but rather on the slow-moving and obsolete inventory.

RETURN ON ASSETS—NABISCO AND AMERICAN STORES

Nabisco's Vice President for Customer Development, Joseph Andraski, says, "We've been focusing on the supply chain since the late 1970s." Operating under the concept of continuous improvements, Nabisco has eliminated operations that it once owned, including truck fleets and warehouses, and now uses public warehouses and fills trucks with goods made by several manufacturers who use the same building for storage.

For example, it has partnered with 20 manufacturers to serve American Stores, a West Coast customer. The result has been a 30 percent reduction in the inventory of products supplied by these manufacturers. With this system, American Stores has also seen its orders filled 99 percent of the time as opposed to the previous figure of 95 percent.

"This is a commonsense way to do business," states Andaski, "and we're going to see a lot more of it."

—*Fortune*, November 9, 1998

"Employees are a company's most valuable asset." How often have we heard that? Although it may seem that it is said far too much, in reality, it is not said enough. It is something that tends to be lost among profit and loss margins, and it should not be. When a company begins viewing its employees as assets, then that company can begin to maximize their participation in its operations and it successes. An effective means of maximizing their participation is to realize the value of their intellectual capital. Knowledge is a prize commodity in today's marketplace to the point that many workers are now being called "knowledge workers." Companies should exploit this capital, while also making sure that their employees have been provided with the tools to harness the energy of Change and adapt to its results.

Continuous improvement is one of the most effective ways to maximize employee participation. As Oliver Cromwell said, "He who stops being better stops being good." If a company and its employees are constantly looking for ways to improve the entire supply chain and realize that nothing in this world is finite, then that company and its supply chain will achieve the ultimate goal: Peak-to-Peak Performance and lasting success. That is the epitome of an SCS organization.

IMPROVED CUSTOMER SATISFACTION

Customer satisfaction is the output of SCS. It is also the means by which the effectiveness of SCS is measured. Customer satisfaction means being easy to do business with, conforming to customer promises, and responding to customer needs. In other words, it is an ongoing, escalating process of meeting requirements and exceeding expectations.

Implementing SCS creates companies that are responsive to the customer's needs through customization. They understand value-added activity. They also understand the issue of flexibility and how to meet ever-changing customer requirements. They completely comprehend the meaning of high quality and strive to provide high value.

MASS CUSTOMIZATION—MERCEDES-BENZ US INTERNATIONAL

Mercedes-Benz US International (MBUSI), a division of DaimlerChrysler, in Vance, Alabama, builds the Mercedes M-Class all-activity vehicles (AAV). MBUSI is using mass customization to meet skyrocketing demands for their vehicles. MBUSI has redesigned their production system for this mass customization, because of the 300 cars produced each day in 1998, often only two were identical.

The system is set up so that each order becomes an independent project with its own Bill of Materials (BOM). An assembler models the assembly line and operations, and the assembly control module determines what needs to be performed for each order and when, calculating parts required for assembly. These requirements are fed to core components for procurement and inventory management. The assembly module also serves as a Manufacturing Execution System (MES) for vehicle orders because it releases the orders and tells each assembly station what parts to install for each vehicle order. Once the AAV is manufactured, the core components are notified to make inventory and supplier payment data available. MBUSI also uses what it calls a "floating stock reorder point." An order to replenish is written in advance, but it is not sent to the supplier until the items are needed.

MBUSI's system streamlines the plant's supply chain, and is projected to increase production by 20 percent this year, from 65,000 to 80,000 units, while minimizing costs and maximizing ROA.

—*Manufacturing Systems*, August 1999

MAXIMIZED SPEED

As I think about the demands for speed, I see a direct correlation between them and a lesson I learned recently. My son and I began off-road motorcycle riding in 1998. By May 1999, he had ridden quite a bit and was pretty good. I, however, had ridden approximately ten hours and my proficiency did not approach his. Undaunted, when he suggested we participate in an off-road trip in the Sequoia National Forest he had discovered on the Internet, I agreed.

We flew to California and met our tour group, which consisted of national champions, young, strong riders, great riders, and Jimmy and me. Jimmy proved to be a natural and was soon going up and down the mountains with the best riders. I was another story. I was 20 years older than the other riders, I was 12,000 feet above sea level, I had ten hours of motorcycle experience, and I was in the mountains.

After the first day, Chris Stewart, a three-time, national off-road motorcycle champion, sat down with me and made three observations:

1. He was a more experienced motorcycle rider than me.
2. He knew the mountains and had more experience riding off-road than me.
3. He had fallen off a motorcycle more than me and had many more broken bones and injuries as a result of these falls than me.

He then said, "Ride fast! If you go slow, you will fall. The steeper the incline, the bumpier the road, and the faster you must ride or you will fall."

"If you go slow, you will fall," applies equally to business as it does to off-road motorcycle riding. Companies, particularly those traveling over steep inclines and bumpy roads, must be able to "ride fast." To BTO, to respond to the customer, to be quick. A company that implements SCS will be able to do this, as well as fill orders quickly. They will see response times reduced, lead times reduced, and they will respond quickly to the marketplace.

MAXIMIZING SPEED—THOMSON CONSUMER ELECTRONICS

In 1998, Thomson Consumer Electronics of Indianapolis, which makes and markets RCA, GE, and ProScan products, launched a program to reduce the production department's assembly steps by 75 percent, with a focus on eliminating the steps that are common only to a few models. The company put in place a plan to assemble "generic" television sets with a few differentiating features until they approached completion. Then, when customer orders came in, the sets would be finished in a series of steps that add features unique to each model.

This strategy is called "postponement," and PC manufacturers practice it daily. This is only one of several plans Thomson has to reduce its response time from a few months to only one month. Production planning is now based on one-month sales forecasts from its customers, and it is now receiving orders and shipping goods weekly rather than monthly.

—*Fortune*, November 9, 1998

REDUCED COSTS

Companies must reduce costs or their supply chains will fail. Industry publications are filled with articles on how to reduce costs and stories about companies that have reduced costs, but where are the articles on reducing costs within the supply chain? Did a company's cost reductions result in reductions in the cost of the supply chain meeting customer requirements? Cost reductions within a link are only of value if they also reduce costs in the supply chain. Transportation costs, acquisition costs, distribution costs, inventory carrying costs, reverse logistics costs, packaging costs, etc., must all be scrutinized to assure the lowest supply chain costs are achieved, and then further reduced. SCS is about providing higher customer satisfaction and providing greater value while reducing supply chain costs and thus growing the supply chain profitability.

INTEGRATED SUPPLY CHAIN

SCS is all about using partnerships and communication to integrate the supply chain. SCS integrates the supply chain and focuses it on the ultimate customer. SCS links work together in true partnerships where all links care more about the supply chain than they do themselves as they realize their individual success is based upon the success of the total chain. This integration demands a new level of communication that is truly real-time and instantaneous throughout the supply chain. This integration of links and communications characterizes SCS and will provide the oneness required for the supply chain to respond quickly as a single entity to the challenges and opportunities of tomorrow.

MAKE IT HAPPEN

In summary, supply chains that adopt a synthesized approach are going to have major successes. Organizations that do not move beyond SCM will fail. To make SCS happen, it is important to be armed with that knowledge as well as the realization that there will be resistance to it. Executives will say, "I don't need to do this because none of my competition is doing it."

The answer to such objections is a quote from Yogi Berra, who said, "If you come to a fork in the road, take it." And that's what I say to you. Seize the initiative. Make SCS happen. The following chapters will show you how.

6

THE CHARACTERISTICS OF SCS AND WHAT IT IS NOT

"One cannot do right in one department of life whilst he is occupied in doing wrong in any other department. Life is an individual whole."

—Gandhi

A news brief in the October 1999 issue of *Logistics* discussed a recent survey of 750 logistics and supply chain executives. When asked what factors would affect the growth and development of logistics, one-third of the executives surveyed replied, "Supply chain integration." This is an amazing response, when you think about it. For years, logistics and supply chain professionals have focused on link optimization, not integration of the supply chain. Then, suddenly, out of the blue, they are announcing, "We have to do it."

A reason for this may stem from the fact that logistics and SCM are not serving to integrate the supply chain. The supply chain

Integration that interests these executives can, however, be accomplished through SCS. This chapter examines the differences between SCS, logistics, and SCM; describes the five characteristics of SCS; discusses what it is not; and introduces the eight core competencies of SCS.

LOGISTICS

Logistics focuses on the internal coordination of materials management (raw materials), material flow through production (work in progress), and physical distribution (finished goods). In other words, logistics begins with the need to order raw materials and ends when the finished goods are shipped. Change or turbulence in the supply chain from either suppliers or customers is viewed as a major irritant and efforts are put forth to minimize the effects. Historically, logistics has never looked at true Integration or the issue of Change; its focus is internal.

The difference between logistics and SCS can be summed up by the end paragraph of a *Logistics Management & Distribution Report* editorial. In his November 1, 1999, "Viewpoint" column, Peter Bradley, Editor-in-Chief, wrote about why the Council of Logistics Management (CLM) invited Canadian climber Jamie Clarke to speak during its annual conference held in October 1999 in Toronto. He pointed out that the logistics planning for a Mount Everest expedition begins three years before the target date and that the logistics for that can rival the demands of logistics managers.

Bradley noted that, in his speech, Clarke asserted that it is essential that climbers on a mountaineering expedition "focus, focus, focus." Bradley then wrote, "That's not a bad reminder for logistics managers or anyone who finds it hard to concentrate on one thing when a hundred things demand attention. I'm going to have a sign made up and hang it in my office. It summarizes well, I think, the way to approach each day. It will read: 'One rung at a time.'"

"One rung at a time" is analogous to "link optimization." Seeing a rung as a vital part of a ladder is good, but for the climb up the ladder to be effective, the whole ladder must be considered. If you focus on one rung, you may not know when to stop or how much farther you have to climb. If you focus on just one link, then you will miss the rest of the chain. SCS ensures that the supply chain flows smoothly and effectively without missing a link or causing a delay.

SCM

SCM is a logistics approach to integrating many links of the supply chain by optimizing each link while attempting to control change. A commonly accepted definition is "the delivery of enhanced customer and economic value through synchronized management of the flow of physical goods from sourcing to consumption." At first glance this seems to be a definition of SCS, but in reality, the way SCM is practiced is to view the flow of physical goods from sourcing to consumption within a link of the chain. Unlike SCS, SCM does not emphasize that the supply chain is a whole and therefore must be viewed holistically.

SCM is a step beyond logistics because it maintains that it is unacceptable to view logistics as an individual link. SCM emphasizes that the integration of many links in the supply chain is important and will result in the elimination of waste. However, the focus of SCM is the optimization of each link to ensure the proper supply of links further down the supply chain. SCM asserts that Change must be managed, which can be translated as "controlled." In the SCM philosophy, it is the control of all deviations from the original plan that allows link optimization (in theory) to contribute to the optimization of the whole supply chain.

In addition to this link optimization challenge, the SCM philosophy that Change can be managed and controlled is without foundation. To repeat a statement from an earlier chapter, Change cannot be managed or controlled.

SCS

SCS is a holistic, continuous improvement process of ensuring customer satisfaction from the original raw material provider to the ultimate finished product consumer. SCS is the synthesis of the supply chain where synthesis is the integration, the unification, and the bringing together of the supply chain links to form a whole. SCS has No Boundaries. It also recognizes that competition in today's marketplace is not company vs. company, but supply chain vs. supply chain, and that sometimes companies that were once like fighting sisters and brothers are now allies in the war between supply chains.

Just as SCM picks up where logistics leaves off, so does SCS pick up where SCM leaves off. While SCM results in link optimization, SCS results in the synthesis and integration of the total integrated pipeline from a customer perspective. Also, where SCM implies a static, controlled environment, SCS harnesses the energy of Change to address the turbulence of the marketplace to achieve true continuous improvement.

What exists, then, is a progression of thought and the corresponding improvements of performance from logistics to SCM to SCS. Performance does improve when a move is made from logistics to SCM. However, performance improves even more after a move from SCM to SCS (Figure 6.1). The five characteristics of SCS discussed below help explain why.

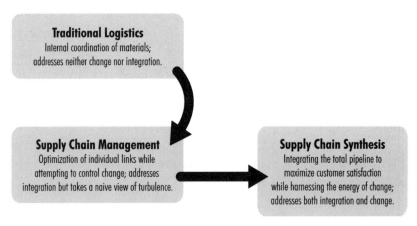

FIGURE 6.1: THE PROGRESSION FROM LOGISTICS TO SCS

WELL-DEFINED PROCESS

SCS is a well-defined process that is understood by all links along the supply chain. "Well-defined" is considered in terms of the entire, complete supply chain. For example, if only two links of the supply chain are well defined, it cannot be expected to net the same results that would occur if the entire supply chain is integrated. Links A and B may have learned the benefits of SCS and, as a result, gained competitive advantage, but if they do not integrate links C and D, then the competitive advantage of the overall supply chain will be lessened.

Those who practice SCS will see that it is important to consider every aspect of the supply chain and understand how each process fits, interacts, and integrates. Otherwise, critical information will be lost or an important link will be missing and all will be lost. An excellent visualization of this is to consider your supply chain as if it were Y2K. No matter how much money was spent on upgrading computer systems so that they were Y2K compliant, the failure of one little chip somewhere could have brought down power grids, telecommunications systems, and banking systems. Those who wrote the files to ready systems for Y2K had to keep this fact in mind. And you must do the same when considering SCS.

INTEGRATED PROCESS

Before SCS, the supply chain focus was on optimizing links. That's selfish. It can be compared to cheering on the offense of a football team while booing its defense. It doesn't make sense. A team needs all players to work together to win a ballgame. Even Michael Jordan, in his early days with the Bulls, and despite his high scoring, couldn't win games alone. He needed teamwork. Michael had learned well the value of teamwork in college. When the team also realized the importance of teamwork, the Bulls became NBA champions.

SCS is an integrated process where selfishness is not allowed. This includes eliminating silos and focusing all links on customer satisfaction. To eliminate silos, we synthesize the whole from the original link to the ultimate customer. That's how all links become focused on continuous improvement of the chain. When this is achieved, we have accomplished SCS and created a supply chain with No Boundaries.

HARNESSING THE ENERGY OF CHANGE

SCS is a process where all involved understand the energy of change and have a desire to harness this energy for the competitive advantage of the total pipeline. This involves courage and innovation. By harnessing change we can turn it into an asset for the total supply chain. Instead of thinking, "I want to improve my link," you may have to think, "Tradeoffs within my link might be what are needed to improve the supply chain."

To illustrate this point, I'll return to Michael Jordan. In many cases, sports fans remember him as being the one who shot the winning basket in so many games. But the beauty of Michael Jordan as a player is the fact that he also recognized when a teammate had a better chance of scoring than he, and he would pass the ball to him. Michael could have taken the shot and gotten the glory, but for the sake of the win, he would give up the ball. Michael is a true competitor and knows that there is plenty of glory for all in getting the win. Sometimes you have to give up your link perspective for the sake of the chain and the sake of the win.

NO INFORMATION DELAYS

SCS is a process that will not accept information delays. SCS requires true partnerships and an integration of information throughout the supply chain. If a link is slowing down information flow, it must be removed from the chain and replaced with an alternative.

Communication delays are as bad as link optimization. To meet today's demands for speed, we not only need for organizations to do the right thing, but we also need for each organization to let all other links know what they are doing quickly. The analogy "the chain is only as strong as its weakest link," becomes "SCS is only as quick as its slowest link." Communication thus becomes key.

With SCM, the progression of knowledge is linear. A link talks to one link, which talks to the next, which talks to the next, and so forth. It is similar to the game of Gossip—the one where one person begins by whispering into a neighbor's ear and this continues until the end, when the last person says the phrase out loud. Inevitably, that phrase is a mutant form of what was originally said.

With SCS, the entire chain is communicating simultaneously. There is no linearity. Instead, the communication is robust and involves simultaneous communication via the Internet. Without accuracy and speed in communications, SCS cannot work. Therefore, communication is a core competency of SCS. Anything that delays communication along the supply chain must be eliminated or replaced.

SUPPLY CHAIN PERFORMANCE

With SCS, partnerships are critical, not only link-to-link, but in the total supply chain. SCS is a continuous improvement process focused on achieving total supply chain performance excellence with the criteria presented in Chapter 5—ROA, customer satisfaction, speed, costs, and integration. Because the supply chain focuses on these five performance criteria, competitive advantage and true supply chain excellence will be achieved.

THE VALUE OF CROSSDOCKING

Crossdocking is receiving and processing goods for reshipping in the shortest time possible, with minimum handling and no storage time. It is a practice that has proven ROI. The beauty of the crossdocking methodology is also that it is not industry discriminate: Wholesalers love it for pushing time-sensitive, fast-moving, sale, and promotional merchandise. Distributors use it to consolidate freight; general and retail distribution is enhanced, especially when door-to-store transport is possible (i.e., an out-bound trailer at the shipping dock for each store serviced by the facility).

Crossdocking obviously benefits the single link, but how does this benefit the entire supply chain? Think in terms of handling costs. Less handling means more accuracy, less probability of product damage, less wear on material handling equipment, and less labor. The supply chain is paying less and assuming less risk with every SKU crossdocked. Ultimately, however, think in terms of customer responsiveness. You're effectively bypassing storage and orderpicking and going directly to shipping with product—how much more responsive can you be? Crossdocking provides the ultimate in speed through links of the supply chain.

WHAT THESE CHARACTERISTICS DEMONSTRATE

The characteristics of SCS demonstrate that SCS is not SCM. SCM is an approach focused on link optimization. It is not a process; *it clearly has boundaries and it has not netted competitive advantage.*

SCS also is not Demand Chain Management, Demand Network Management, Demand Network Integration, Value Chain Management, Customer-Driven Demand Network; nor is it Supply Chain Coordination, Supply Chain Integration, or Demand/Supply Chain Management. These are all names for link approaches rather than for a holistic process. The section that follows describes these linear approaches and compares them to SCS.

THE LIMITS OF WHERE WE HAVE BEEN

Demand Chain Management handles order management, distribution logistics, inventory replenishment, and demand planning. Like SCM, its focus is the link; it looks downstream and focuses on only the demand aspect of the supply chain.

Demand Network Management is similar to Demand Chain Management except that it has a marketing component within the demand planning module that may or may not contribute to the competitive advantage of the supply chain.

Demand Network Integration is similar to Demand Network Management, but it is broader in that it has a greater real-time response to changes in demand. The same may be said for Customer-Driven Demand Network, but it has a greater awareness of the build-to-order and customization requirements that exist downstream. The Value Chain Management mindset goes a bit further in that it desires to look both at the demand and supply requirements of the supply chain. Unfortunately, Value Chain Management is still an approach, not a process, pursuing optimization instead of meeting the true needs of continuous improvement.

At first glance, Supply Chain Coordination is alluring. Coordination is an integral component of supply chain design. Also, well-coordinated discrete activities are more efficient than disjointed independent action. However, Supply Chain Coordination still allows the slowest or weakest link to determine overall operating efficiency and speed of the supply chain. Most importantly, Supply Chain Coordination does not mean Supply Chain Integration and it is still based upon link optimization.

Declaring that Supply Chain Integration is not SCS may seem confusing. After all, since the first pages of this book, I have been emphasizing how important Integration is in SCS. However, although Supply Chain Integration is viewed as producing greater technological innovation, leveraged knowledge, shared business risks, shorter cycle times (both production and design), and integration of production planning, it does not provide the tools for harnessing change.

Remember the riverbanks, Integration and Change? Without both, you only have a puddle. Supply Chain Integration is a puddle because it lacks the riverbank called Change. SCS is a river that flows between Integration and Change.

Demand/Supply Chain Management is similar to Value Chain Management in that it is the combination of what is seen as traditional supply components (e.g., purchasing, inventory management, MES, MRP, and process control) with what is seen as traditional demand components (e.g., demand management, planning, scheduling, sales, order fulfillment). Like SCM, Demand/Supply Chain Management is a logistics concept, and it still focuses on link optimization.

DEMAND/SUPPLY CHAIN MANAGEMENT OBSTACLES

In July 1999, *Demand & Supply Chain Management* reported although companies such as Armstrong World-wide, Procter & Gamble, Quaker Oats, VF Corporation, Wal-Mart, Amazon.com, and Wegmans view Demand/Supply Chain Management as one of the leading sources of competitive advantage, they also face obstacles when putting it into practice. The article reports that gaining substantial performance improvements in supply/demand chain management has met with certain obstacles, including culture and critical mass.

Cultural obstacles are based on the inherent distrust between buyers and sellers. Since trust, interdependence, and reliable information systems are critical components of Demand/Supply Chain Management and adversarial relationships still exist, it seems that Demand/Supply Chain Management does not offer solutions to this mistrust.

Many companies object to investing in new systems and processes that require similar investments from other companies along the supply chain. They want the other organizations to invest first. Demand/Supply Chain Management fails to encourage the partnerships necessary to overcome such resistance.

NO BOUNDARIES

SCM, Demand Change Management, Demand Network Management, Demand Network Integration, Customer-Driven Demand Network, Value Chain Management, Supply Chain Coordination, Supply Chain Integration, and Demand/Supply Chain Management all share one characteristic: Every one of these approaches has boundaries. SCS removes these boundaries. In SCS, there are partnerships, not only link to link, but in the total chain to accomplish the objective of the integrated supply chain. A synthesized supply chain has No Boundaries.

EIGHT CORE COMPETENCIES

Changing the way your business works is a challenge. SCS can meet that challenge. The eight core competencies of SCS will allow you to achieve SCS success. These eight core competencies are

1. Understanding Change
2. Understanding Peak-to-Peak Performance
3. Understanding Customer Satisfaction
4. Understanding Total Operations
5. Understanding Manufacturing Synthesis
6. Understanding Distribution Synthesis
7. Understanding SCS Partnerships
8. Understanding SCS Communications.

These eight competencies are the subject of the next eight chapters.

7

SCS AND CHANGE

"Adapt or perish, now as ever, is Nature's inexorable imperative."

—H. G. Wells

Lefty Gomez was one of the greatest pitchers in the history of the New York Yankees. In 1934, for example, he won 26 games and lost only five. However, as time went on, he lost his edge.

Joe McCarthy, the Yankees' manager, counseled him. "I don't think you're throwing as hard as you need to."

Lefty replied, "You're wrong, Joe. I'm throwing twice as hard. But the ball isn't going as fast."

That's exactly what is happening in business today. Companies are working hard, very hard, but the product doesn't flow as fast as it should.

Consider the following quote from *Harvard Business Review*: "More and more companies are trying to make a fundamental change in the way they operate. For years, they've struggled with growing competition by introducing improvements (or at least improvement programs) into every function and process. But the competitive pressures keep getting worse, the pace of

Change keeps accelerating, and companies keep pouring executive energy into the search for ever higher levels of quality, service, and overall business agility. The treadmill moves faster, companies work harder, results improve slowly or not at all."[1] What ails these companies is not Change per se, but the fact that they try to manage Change. They also attempt to pursue Change without understanding its science. This chapter discusses both, and explains why Understanding Change is one of the eight core competencies of SCS.

YOU CANNOT MANAGE CHANGE

Change, despite the declarations of many business leaders and writers, is not manageable. Organizations can attempt to drive markets and customers in a specific direction, but the climate of commerce is as unpredictable as tomorrow's weather forecast. Managing Change cannot be accomplished. You can ride the wave of Change, but you cannot tell the wave how high or challenging it must be.

Not long ago, a flyer advertising a seminar on Managing Change appeared on my desk. With curiosity, I picked it up and looked to see if the person leading that seminar had a beard. Why? Because I was looking for a picture of God, for only God can manage or control Change. Sadly, the person leading the seminar had no beard, but I was not surprised. I really did not expect that I would be attending a seminar led by God. What was even more disappointing was the fact that this beardless wonder claimed he knew how to manage Change.

This traditional assumption that Change can be managed is not only false, it is also contradictory. To manage means control. In today's dynamic environment, people cannot control Change.

Change can be good or bad. If you try to manage Change or resist it, you are history. Seventy percent of all organizational change fails, not because the change was bad, but because the method for introducing the change was badly orchestrated and therefore created resistance. If you harness the energy of Change, you will make history. As John F. (Jack) Welch, CEO of GE, said in a 1993 interview, "You've got to be on the cutting edge of change." His advice: "Get all the facts out. Give people the rationale for change, laying it out in the clearest terms."

This is not too far from what I believe. I believe that if the energy of Change is harnessed with the intent of improving the well-being of an entire supply chain, then it should be embraced and used. Tolerating Change is not enough and managing Change is not possible. The power of Change must be harnessed.

SEARS—A STORY OF RESISTANCE

For the 12 years (1980-1992) he was CEO of Sears, Ed Brennan instituted a number of changes that should have been profitable. He sold the Sears Tower, instituted the acceptance of other credit cards along with the Sears credit card, launched Brand Central, diversified into financial services, and invested a great deal to launch the Discover Card. He also simplified logistics, focused on selling women's apparel, began streamlining the buying organization, and created specialized Sears automotive, home-furnishing, and home-improvement stores.

Unfortunately, it is Brennan's successor, Arthur Martinez, who is well-known for revitalizing the retail side of Sears. Why? Because Brennan failed to understand the pain of Change and the resistance it can create. Store management teams, upset and angry about layoffs, decentralization, and threats of more layoffs, alienated customers with their inconsistent merchandising, poor service, and frequent out-of-stock conditions. Brennan's command-and-control attitude, conveyed by a hard line and disagreeable edicts, did not motivate employees to Change. Not only that, but he did not do anything to correct the perception among his management team or employees that Change was a bad thing. He never told his employees what was changing and why.

THE SCIENCE OF CHANGE

The fast and discontinuous world of Change is a science that must be understood. The science of Change begins with the relationship between Change and pain. Pain usually accompanies Change; this is perfectly natural. On a personal level, pain is a body's signal that it is being harmed or harming itself. In business, it is a sign that the organization is harming itself. This pain may be felt in quality problems, competitiveness, customer satisfaction, turnover, and so on. The challenge, then, is the organizational response to pain and its resilience. How does the organization absorb and respond to Change?

If the speed of Change is less than an organization's resilience, then it can harness the energy of Change and become successful. If the speed of Change is greater, then the pain of Change is too much. So, since the organization cannot control the speed of Change, it is vital to build up its resilience and the ability to manage its resilience capacity.

RESILIENCE

Resilience is the ability to bounce. If someone holds a ball at shoulder height and drops it, if the ball bounces back up to that person's shoulder, a mechanical engineer would say that it has a resilience of one. If the ball does not bounce at all, then it has a resilience of zero. If it bounces back twice as high, then it has a resilience of two.

Everyone has resilience. It is the ability to absorb Change, and it can be measured in points. For example, if I have 1000 personal absorption points, I might decide to allocate 700 points to my work, profession, and company while 200 points go to my family, 50 to my church, and 50 points to country and community. If my business is doing well, and it is growing with more work than capacity, I may actually be using 850 absorption points rather than 700. Meanwhile, at home, I have a wife who wants me to slow down, I have a daughter who was a microbiologist with Bayer until I convinced her to join my company, a younger daughter who wants to get married, but is not impressed with her boyfriends, and a 15-year-old son who is doing everything that 15- and 16-year-old boys do at that time of life. So, it appears that I am using 350 absorption points on my family rather than the 200 I allocated.

What does this mean? It means that if I come in to work and my administrative assistant says, "Jim, that meeting you have planned for 9:30 has been changed to 10:00 because one of the principals who is supposed to call in cannot get to a phone until that time," I hit the roof. I say, "What do you mean, it's 10:00? Don't they know the schedule? I can't be changing things around like this! I've got work to do. I've got to make this happen in a timely manner!" Then I look at myself and say, "What an idiot. I am a complete dipstick. What a jerk."

What makes me like that? After all, the change in meeting time is probably about one-tenth of an absorption point. It barely registers. However, if I have no points left, then a tenth of a point is more than I can give.

The science of Change involves careful consideration of these absorption points. It is based on building resilience capacity, both personal and organizational. If I am successful in building my resilience capacity, then I can then apply it to someone else's resilience capacity. Before long, I can build the organization's resilience capacity so that it can harness the energy of Change at the current rate of Change.

BUILDING PERSONAL AND ORGANIZATIONAL RESILIENCE CAPACITY

There are three guidelines for building personal resilience capacity:

1. Raising resilience capacity comes both from increased pain management and remedy management.
2. Lowering the effort needed to harness the energy of change requires an organization to deal with the perceived levels of certainty and control.
3. The energy to deal with change comes from having a balanced life.

Raising organizational resilience capacity to harness the energy of Change is based on three factors:

1. Organizations must increase their understanding of the

positive effects of change and the negative effects of not changing.

2. Organizations must increase certainty and control.
3. Organizations must be assured that their personnel are in alignment with their focus of the future.

An organization that considers these factors when building resilience capacity also understands the four "Boomerang Principles."

Here is the first principle: What comes back will be exactly the same. When you throw a boomerang, the same boomerang returns. An organization that harnesses the energy of Change will mirror the feelings, thoughts, and commitment put forth by its leaders.

The second principle is: What comes back will always be more than what was put forth. A boomerang gains momentum and returns at a faster speed. In an organization that harnesses the energy of Change, the synergy that evolves acts as a multiplier for the evolution of renewal progress, improvement, growth, and success.

The third principle is this: Results are always obtained after the investment is made. A boomerang will not return if it is not thrown. How long it takes to return depends on various complex factors and is difficult to predict. It will return, however, and an organization that has harnessed the energy of change recognizes that fact.

The fourth principle is: Benefits will be positive only if the organization's leader knows how to throw the boomerang. It takes practice to know how to throw a boomerang. For an organization to harness the energy of Change, the leader must know how to nurture the process and overcome difficulties. With effective, insightful leadership, an organization will find No Boundaries between their strategic vision and their successful reality.

ORGANIZATIONS THAT UNDERSTAND CHANGE

An organization that understands Change has a number of identifying characteristics. For one, each employee has clearly defined responsibilities, accountabilities, roles, and identities. However, at the same time, not one of those employees is ever heard saying, "That's not part of my job description." That's because the organization does not shackle its staff to outmoded ways of thinking to which they can cling when Change occurs. Instead, the expectations of each employee are delineated and are altered only after conference and mutual agreement.

Another characteristic is continuity and flexibility in the organization's purpose without inflexibility. Organizational focus is proactively, not reactively, maintained. These organizations may reconceptualize missions and goals, but they still keep their vision in sight. Also, the focus of employees within the organization is consistent with the organization's focus. However, everyone in the organization understands the necessity of Change. All employees believe that Change will benefit them both personally and professionally. As Lawrence Bossidy, the CEO of AlliedSignal said in an interview with *Fortune*, "Scaring people isn't the answer. You try to appeal to them. The more they understand why you want Change, the easier it is to commit to it. And they must believe they can win."

An organization that understands Change practices effective communication, since communication is vital to the health of a company that harnesses the energy of Change. Businesses are often full of secrets. Their executives do not believe that employees need to know strategic plans and paths of the organization. You will not see that in an organization that understands Change. As Bossidy says, "Candor is a way to treat people with dignity. You go out there and answer questions as directly as you can. Sometimes it's difficult, but it earns you credibility." In those organizations, employees are encouraged to participate in and provide feedback to organizational changes. Information flows through the organization in a timely manner.

WHY UNDERSTANDING CHANGE IS A CORE COMPETENCY OF SCS

Changes in the fundamental structure of businesses create substantial changes in the ways employees work within that business. Some of these changes are direct and can be handled quickly, such as repairing a failing HVAC system or hiring a new employee. Others are indirect and tend to affect an organization's strategy and competitive advantage. They can reduce market share, alter the distribution network, and cause the company to rethink customer needs.

For example, an environmental testing firm sold its products domestically for many years. The manufacturing staff, therefore, only wired and calibrated equipment for the U.S. market. During a lull in the domestic market, the firm decided to sell its product internationally.

The sales team then made its biggest sale in the history: an Australian firm bought entire lines of its product. Unfortunately, this sale, which had so much potential, fell flat. Why? Because no one told the manufacturing staff that Australia's electricity runs on 220 volts, not 110 volts. The manufactured goods did not work in Australia: they had been manufactured for a 110 volt market. Somewhere along the pipeline, someone forgot to relay key information.

As the above story also demonstrates, the supply chain is not in a steady state. By expanding the reach of its product, the company needed a different supply chain, but instead they relied on the one they had always used. In other words, a great supply chain today may be terrible just six weeks from now. We live in a constant state of whitewater, and SCS responds to this. SCS recognizes that Change affects all aspects of the pipeline and fosters preparation for the affects of Change. SCS is also a process of continuous improvement that embraces and harnesses Change. It permanently rekindles individual creativity and responsibility and creates a transformation of a company's internal and external relationships—relationships with No Boundaries.

To embrace and harness Change, you must understand it. That is why understanding Change is one of the core competencies of SCS.

8

SCS AND PEAK-TO-PEAK PERFORMANCE

"Once you are labeled 'the best' you want to stay up there, and you can't do it by loafing around. If I don't keep changing, I'm history."

—Larry Bird

To many people, success is the ultimate goal. It is hard to associate success with failure. Yet, peak performance is often the beginning of failure. As radio commentator Walter Winchell once observed, "Nothing recedes like success." How can this be? Doesn't success breed success? That's what we've all been told. Also, we've all been told at one time that the pilgrims were the first English-speaking settlers of America. Neither is true.

Winston Churchill said, "Success is rarely final." Benjamin Franklin said, "Success has ruined many a man." Now, they were on the right track.

The natural order of life is peak-to-valley-to-peak-to-valley, and so on. This is like a basketball team that exhausts itself chipping away at a large deficit and consequently lacks the momentum to pull out the victory. The peak represents success and the valley that follows, failure. This can be explained by a quote from Henry Kissinger, who said, "Every success only buys an admission ticket to a more difficult problem." Analogous to this statement is the American education system. A student starts at a lower level and works him or herself up to the next level, and then the process starts all over again. A student begins in the lower grade of middle school, for example, and as he or she learns and succeeds in that grade, he or she is promoted. Success! In the last year of middle school, the student is on the top of the peak. Success at that level promotes the student out of middle school and into high school, and then what happens? The student is back at the bottom of the valley again, and he or she has to climb back to the top. Success is measured by a diploma which sends the student either out into the world for that first job or on to college—either of which puts them back on the bottom, and the climb begins again.

You can circumvent this process with Peak-to-Peak Performance, which is the second core competency of SCS. In fact, if you don't design your supply chain for Peak-to-Peak Performance, success will ruin you. You will follow success with failure. This chapter addresses Peak-to-Peak Performance, refutes the myths of consistency and success, and explains why Peak-to-Peak Performance is a core competency of SCS.

PEAK-TO-PEAK PERFORMANCE

As the founder, chairman, and president of an engineering-based consulting firm, I have taken my organization from success to failure, from failure to success, and from success to success. Through my experiences, I have determined the four evolutions of a company:

1. Fail/fail
2. Fail/succeed
3. Succeed/fail
4. Succeed/Succeed.

Fail/fail is usually a vicious cycle that keeps destroying confidence until the ultimate failure occurs: The person stops trying. He or she finds solace in Irv Mayer's philosopy: "If at first you don't succeed, try, try again. Then give up. No use being a damn fool about it." Most people do not have the patience of Thomas Edison, who considered each unsuccessful result as a step closer to success, or Abraham Lincoln, who failed repeatedly in business and politics before rising to save our nation. The nature of business is more realistic: Repeated failures are a luxury most companies cannot afford.

What puts companies in a fail/fail cycle? They do not learn from their mistakes. As the saying goes, "Insanity is doing the same thing over and over and expecting different results." There are many companies like this. You do not hear much about them because they never succeed. Or you hear that someone has bought them out before they went anywhere. Often these companies are led by CEOs who will not admit they make mistakes and run around blaming others in the company for their failures. Such companies enter the fail/fail cycle quickly.

Fail/succeed is the pattern of people who learn from their mistakes to overcome setbacks. The same may be said for companies like a retail giant that, after suffering failure, hired a new CEO who looked at his successor's failures, saw the good in them, recognized the bad, and then began working with his management teams to eliminate the bad. Currently, the retail chain is a dominant player in its market. Those who view failure as a challenge can turn adversity into the motivation to succeed.

Succeed/fail is the most common progression for people and organizations. Consider the "sophomore jinx," which can turn a sensational freshman or rookie into an average player during the second season. In the entertainment field, most movie sequels fail to match the excellence of the originals, and in literature, an author's second book may not measure up the first. Examples of companies that have experienced succeed/fail are numerous. You see their "going out of business" signs every day or read that they've filed for bankruptcy in the newspaper or hear that they are being sold. I can name examples from almost every industry: automotive, retail, publishing, printing, pharmaceutical and healthcare, and so forth.

Succeed/succeed is the final step in this revolution. An organization that learns the formula to succeed/succeed is like the basketball team that knows how to take the lead and hold on to it. They play to win instead of playing to avoid losing. The key is continuous improvement. A company that practices continuous improvement will remain in the succeed/succeed cycle and will, therefore, achieve Peak-to-Peak Performance. An example of this is Intel, a company that refuses to rest on their processor laurels and are always seeking ways to improve their business methods.

SUCCEED/SUCCEED—INTEL

Intel has enjoyed huge success and profit from its microprocessors, the most well-known of which is the Pentium. However, in 1995, as Intel saw the life cycle of its products decreasing from eight years for the 386 series to a much shorter period, the company decided to examine the sales-order computer system they were using. The system kept track of pricing, orders, delivery, and inventory management. Orders from the U.S., Japan, Asia, and Europe were handled on separate systems and then rolled together so that they could be tracked on the domestic system. This setup was unable to keep track of inventory and was not Y2K-compliant. Intel decided to replace the system with ERP software and managed to install it during a time when Intel's annual revenues were increasing from $18 billion to $26 billion and its employee roster was growing from 40,000 employees to 60,000 employees. After the new system was installed, the company was able to track inventory all over the world, commit it to a customer, and deliver it in three days.

Two years later, Intel decided to halt growing shipping costs before they reached $1 billion (which was the forecast for 2001). It reshuffled its global logistics and directed a major portion of its production flow to three new warehouses located next to airports in Malaysia, the Philippines, and Costa Rica. These facilities are integrated, handling both parts and materials that arrive from suppliers and other Intel plants, and outbound finished chips slated to be delivered to customers. Intel now can guarantee its air-freight contractors full or almost full airplanes, which results in lower freight rates for the company. Intel also redesigned its packaging to nest twice as many cartridges safely in each carton. This saves $1 million per week in shipping costs.

Why did Intel do all this? So that they would continue to succeed instead of failing. They use continuous improvement regularly to make sure that they move from peak-to-peak. So far, it is working.

Peak-to-Peak Performance involves the continuous process of beginning anew and climbing to a new peak, and then the next peak, and the peak after that. It means that a company should not wait for outside factors to force its hand, but instead should innovate on its own terms and prepare for challenges before they arise, while being wary of the naysayers. The process that helps a company move from peak-to-peak is called Revolution, which makes sense when you consider that Peak-to-Peak Performance requires innovation and preparing for challenges before they arise. These are the characteristics of most good revolutionaries. Such succeed/succeed revolutionaries include John Wooden, former coach of the most successful college basketball team of this century, who said, "It's what you learn after you know it all that counts." Another is Jerry Garcia, former leader of the most successful live rock group band of all time. "You don't just want to be considered one of the best," Garcia said. "You want to be considered the only one who does what you do."

SUCCESS CAN BE HAZARDOUS

Success can be hazardous to an organization's health because most organizations cycle through time alternating between the fail/succeed and succeed/fail methods. They begin with a surge of entrepreneurial energy and climb the mountain to success, thus achieving peak performance. They become smug, even arrogant, stop being entrepreneurial, protect their success, decline, and fail. Their performance falls and they find themselves in a valley. Like the retailer I mentioned earlier, they bring in new leadership, reorganize, refresh the entrepreneurial spirit, and once again climb the mountain to success. Once they have reached this peak, the cycle begins again. In fact, this cycle will generally continue over time until an organization loses touch with its own mortality and cycles from a succeed/fail into a fail/fail. Then everyone asks, "What happened? How could such a great company go out of business?"

Another hazard of success is the consistency myth. Many people and organizations believe that since consistency often takes them to the peak, then it will also keep them there. This is just not so. Although consistency is necessary when producing a quality product, it does not necessarily allow the agility needed to adjust to changes. It can often drag a company down to the valley. As Aldous Huxley once said, "Consistency is contrary to nature, contrary to life. The only completely consistent people are the dead." The same is true of organizations. If they are completely consistent, they will be dead.

Business is difficult, and is becoming even more so, with the globalization of economics and the speed of the Internet. In these changing times, a business has two choices. It can cycle through the succeed/fail routine, which, with its barrage of downsizing, rightsizing, restructuring, repositioning, demassing, and reengineering, is the dominant pattern of business today. Or the business may choose to revolutionize the fundamental way it does business and strive to become better than the best, grow, and be successful today, tomorrow, and into the future. It all starts with the realization that today's peak performance is tomorrow's good performance, next week's average performance, and next month's poor performance. It also means realizing that consistency must be pursued or abandoned, depending on a particular situation. Consistency that is bound to the quality of a product and consistency in meeting work schedules should be pursued, but consistency is not always the answer.

SCS AND THE PRINCIPLES OF REVOLUTION

Supply Chain Synthesis is the process of applying the principles of Revolution to the supply chain. Consider the prerequisites for the Revolution that lead to Peak-to-Peak Performance:

1. Commitment to continuous improvement
2. Harnessing the energy of change
3. Motivational leadership
4. Revolutionizing the culture
5. Alignment.

Do you recognize any of these? You should, because the first two in the list above are in my definition of SCS and are covered in other chapters. Let's discuss the other three.

MOTIVATIONAL LEADERSHIP

Although leadership is not a set of traits, true leaders have the following characteristics:

- Integrity—the leader lives and tells the truth
- Credibility—the leader is accountable, genuine, and open
- Enthusiasm—the leader shows his excitement about the future
- Optimism—the leader focuses on success
- Urgency—the leader knows that the only way to impact the future is to act today
- Determination—the leader steps forward to face doubts and uncertainties, to accept risk, to move forward, and to make real his or her understanding that there are No Boundaries between his or her organization and competitive advantage. Leaders act.

Relying on these characteristics, leaders motivate others by the way they communicate, work, and treat others. Leaders recognize the importance of effective communication and they arm people with the certainty and control that allows them to harness the energy of change through direct communication and the sharing of information. When leaders make decisions, they adhere to the "three rights": the *right* decisions at the *right* time communicated to the *right* people. They enjoy their work. Finally, leaders treat others in the way others want to be treated.

Motivational leaders create the environment necessary for SCS. They seek out other motivational leaders in their supply chain partnerships and share skills and knowledge. They also recognize that instantaneous dissemination of information with No Boundaries among partners is critical to the success of SCS.

REVOLUTIONIZING THE CULTURE

Culture is the personality of an organization, but it is also the personality of a supply chain. Any Revolution that tries to change merely the inanimate portions of the supply chain—facilities, equipment, transportation—will fail unless it changes the people involved and how they interact with one another. Revolutionizing a culture is no simple task, for an organization's culture will try to stifle the introduction of a new one. Cultural Revolution also must go beyond simple changes in the cultural manifestations and perceptions, and transform the organization's culture. It must transform the rules, habits, procedures, standards, norms, rewards, language, jargon, stories, expectations, ceremonies, and titles that affect cultural conformance, organizational behavior, and organizational performance. The foundation for this is a shared, consistent vision of where the organization is headed. Everyone must be aligned with a commitment to dynamic consistency, the underlying basis of which is "improve, improve, improve." This means understanding the difference between "change, change, change," and "improve, improve, improve."

Revolutionizing the culture in the supply chain involves more than one organization. Often several corporate cultures are involved. But if the different cultures can align themselves to the vision of continuously improving the ultimate customer's satisfaction, then they can bring about SCS.

ALIGNMENT

An organization achieves alignment when it can accomplish the following:

- Connect its employees' behavior to the mission of the company, turning intentions into actions
- Link teams and processes to the changing needs of customers
- Shape business strategy with real-time information from customers
- Create a culture in which these elements all work together seamlessly.

The same principles apply to an extraorganizational collaboration among supply chain partners. The seamless connection between the producer of raw materials and the ultimate customer is the essence of SCS.

WHY PEAK-TO-PEAK PERFORMANCE IS A CORE COMPETENCY OF SCS

When supply chain partners commit themselves to SCS, they also commit themselves to continuous improvement, harnessing the energy of change, motivational leadership, revolutionizing their cultures, and alignment. They understand that continuous renewal is not a program that ends but rather an ongoing process. They accept that they are the underdogs because they are on top. And finally, they will experience the non-stop evolution with No Boundaries to higher levels of Peak-to-Peak Performance. Peak-to-Peak Performance is critical to the success of SCS and that is why it is a core competency of SCS. At the same time, SCS is also critical to the success of Peak-to-Performance in the increasingly globalized, build-to-order, electronic marketplace.

9

SCS AND TOTAL OPERATIONS

"To a hammer, everything looks like a nail."

—Mark Twain

T he following are examples of problems companies face today:

1. Company A has a SKU explosion that has created a shortage of warehouse space.
2. Company B has a manufacturing capacity problem on a new, hot-selling item.
3. Company C has a customer satisfaction problem.

Now, consider these questions. Should Company A's problem be solved by manufacturing smaller lot sizes or should it be solved by adding square footage to the warehouse? Should the solution for Company B's problem be adding capacity to manufacturing or by increasing yield or by increasing uptime? Should the resolution of Company C's problem be reconfiguring the distribution network or installing a new warehouse management system or by implementing a continuous improvement process?

What are your answers? How did you think these problems should be solved? You may find that your solution has less to do with the problem and more to do with your area of expertise. A warehouse expert would view these problems as warehouse-related. A systems expert would argue that they are systems problems. A maintenance expert would declare that they are maintenance problems. The reality, however, is that to identify and solve these problems, these experts must work with others who have complementary skill sets. The companies must adopt a Total Operations solution—one with No Boundaries. This chapter defines Total Operations and its impact on SCS and explains why Total Operations is a core competency of SCS.

TOTAL OPERATIONS

Total Operations is the integration of the warehouse, logistics, manufacturing, quality, maintenance, organizational excellence, and systems. It is a holistic concept that stretches from the planning of a site through the determination of the correct network to the cultural ties that bind employees to an organization's mission. It is based on collaboration, which has a definite science, both within the organization and without. The internal collaboration consists of teams focused on ongoing, incremental improvements, as well as innovation, communication, and leadership. The external collaboration consists of judicious partnerships with suppliers, vendors, customers, contract manufacturers, and anyone else along the supply chain.

EXTERNAL COLLABORATION—NABISCO AND WEGMAN'S

Nabisco and the Wegman's grocery chain realized that they were both looking for answers to the same question: "How can we maximize profitability for on-the-shelf space for Planters products?" They created a joint forecast to include market activities, initiated replenishment orders from a set forecast, refined the established forecast-replenishment plan to drive the sourcing, production, and transportation plans, and monitored execution against the plans. Planters sales increased by 47 percent and stock availability rose from 92.8 percent to 96.6 percent. Planters and Wegman's clearly understand external collaboration.

By focusing on the whole, a Total Operations view assures an organization

- The correct distribution network
- The correct manufacturing methods
- The correct warehousing methods
- The correct operating systems
- The correct maintenance methods
- The quality to satisfy customers
- The correct process for continuous improvement.

As you can see, the Total Operations view does not focus on one technology or component. That would be like building a house with only a hammer. Building a house takes more than a hammer: It also takes a saw, a ruler, a paint brush, a screw driver, and a variety of other tools. So, too, does building an organization of excellence: There are many parts and no one piece is more important than another. A Total Operations view recognizes this.

TOTAL OPERATIONS AND THE SUPPLY CHAIN

Total Operations is based on the premise that logistics cannot be managed apart from all other operations in a company. Instead, logistics must be integrated with everything else in order to bring harmony to the supply chain. Supply chains are not simply about logistics. They are not simply about distribution. Instead they are about everything that affects operations: inbound and outbound transportation, material handling, preventive and predictive maintenance, statistical process control, manufacturing methods, customer satisfaction, inventory management, production planning, partnerships, teams, information, warehousing methods, etc.—in short, the *entire operation*.

The first time Tompkins installed an SCS environment was ten years ago. A major appliance manufacturer had hired us. We removed their inventory, streamlined procedures, and thus improved customer satisfaction. Everything was functioning like clockwork until a fancy German machine that made the appliance shell went down for two weeks. The fallout was almost catastrophic. New homeowners were unable move into their houses because they didn't have appliances and without them, they could not acquire certificates of occupancy. Dealers were unhappy because there were no products. Eleven days later, the machine was fixed, but the damage had been done.

The president of the company said to me, "Jim, we need to put all of the inventory back in. We will never, ever do that again."

I replied, "Sir, I agree with you. You should never, ever do that again. But you cannot put the inventory back in."

His face got red, and he stood up. "Jim," he said, "What am I going to do without the inventory?"

I said, "You never, ever, ever let that machine go down again. If you can't make sure 100 percent that that's true, then you build a second one and let it sit there looking at the first one, because you can buy ten of those machines cheaper than you can put that inventory and that glut back in the system."

He said, "You're hired."

I said, "Thank you. What's the assignment?"

He answered, "Do maintenance on that machine."

I went back to my company and asked, "Does anyone know how to do maintenance? I don't know how to do it! What are we going to do?"

Of course, I really knew what I had to do, so I did it. I hired someone to do maintenance.

SCS is not possible without understanding maintenance—or quality, manufacturing, logistics, warehousing, organizational excellence, and systems. SCS demands pursuit of excellence in all functional areas—not simply logistics.

To achieve true supply chain excellence, the depth of Total Operations must be spread across the breadth of the supply chain. Again, there should be No Boundaries. If this is not done well, the result will be a never-ending list of unkept commitments that will impact the entire supply chain. This lack of performance will ultimately create poor customer satisfaction and result in the loss of market share for all of the supply chain's links. Therefore, it is critical that all aspects of Total Operations be pursued across all supply chain links and not simply within each link.

WHY TOTAL OPERATIONS IS A CORE COMPETENCY OF SCS

Pursuing Total Operations across all supply chain links demands that

- The distribution network for the supply chain be designed from the perspective of the entire supply chain and not from the perspective of any one link
- The proper manufacturing and warehousing methods be performed in the context of the whole supply chain
- The ultimate customer quality expectations be understood by all links and be the driving force for defining maintenance and quality requirements throughout the supply chain
- All links understand the continuous improvement efforts of other links so that the continuous improvement process is focused on the chain and not the links
- The people throughout the supply chain be aligned and committed to the process of SCS.

Designing the distribution network across the entire supply chain may be achieved through distribution synthesis, which will be addressed more fully in Chapter 12. Basically, distribution synthesis is making sure that the right manufacturing operations and right distribution centers are in the right locations, holding the right amount of inventory, and that the right transportation is being used to fulfill the satisfaction of the customer. When this is done from a link's perspective, this is called logistics. When it is done from a chain's perspective, it is called SCS. It is the harmony that evolves throughout the supply chain by adopting a Total Operations perspective throughout the supply chain that results in true supply chain excellence.

LEADERSHIP QUALITIES FOR THE FUTURE—TOTAL OPERATIONS

A recent survey asked 75 business leaders and potential leaders in the U.S., Europe, and Australia were asked to look five years into the future and define the qualities that will distinguish leaders at that time. The results were the following qualities:

1. Create a shared vision
2. Ensure customer satisfaction
3. Live the values
4. Build teamwork and partnerships
5. Think globally
6. Appreciate cultural diversity
7. Develop and unleash the power of people
8. Anticipate opportunity
9. Achieve competitive advantage
10. Embrace change
11. Share leadership
12. Demonstrate personal mastery
13. Show technological savvy
14. Encourage constructive challenge.

What these leaders did not realize is that their 14 qualities could have been summed up in two words: Total Operations, for they are all part of the Total Operations view. Any leader who has the above characteristics had the ability to pass them on in his or her organization. In so doing, he or she is creating a Total Operations environment.

Manufacturing is no longer a peripheral player in the success of the supply chain. Performing manufacturing and warehousing across the entire supply chain involves manufacturing synthesis, the subject of Chapter 11. Briefly, manufacturing synthesis involves small lot sizes, short lead times, short setup times, and responsive manufacturing—all to be responsive to the needs of the supply chain. It includes warehousing and manufacturing practices driven by the correct systems—Warehouse Management Systems (WMS), Manufacturing Execution Systems (MES), Enterprise Asset Management (EAM), and Advanced Planning and Scheduling Systems (APS)—to achieve manufacturing synthesis.

The correct WMSs (those required by Total Operations) are real-time, bar-code based, Radio-Frequency (RF)-based systems that maximize warehouse performance. The correct MES provides critical information on manufacturing decision-making and enables product engineering to improve on product design through historical repair work tracking. The correct EAM treats asset management as an integrated process, not just automation of a set of administrative tasks. The correct APS is a robust package that provides multi-site control over the manufacturing process, thus strengthening responsiveness and reliability.

What do these correct systems have in common? For one, all of them are necessary for manufacturing synthesis. They also rely on integration and they also do not operate in a vacuum. The truly effective examples integrate and interface with each other, creating an intelligent warehouse where computer systems, material handling equipment, storage equipment, and people form a single, cohesive unit. The Total Operations view sees and understands that the boundaries between manufacturing and warehousing are blurring. So, how does this Total Operations requirement differ from SCS? It doesn't. Neither recognizes boundaries.

The third requirement is part of the Total Operations focus on the ultimate customer. It demands an awareness of the customer up and down and all along the supply chain, as well as an awareness of the customer's definition of quality. Proper maintenance and quality methods and procedures must be in place to protect against breakdown and/or defective products and there must be no buffer that allows interruptions in service to disturb the links in the supply chain. Serving the customer is the foundation of this focus, but what is even more vital is the customer's satisfaction. The formula for this is Customer Satisfaction = Perception of Service – Expectation of Service. Does this sound familiar? It should. This Total Operations requirement is no different from the SCS customer satisfaction requirement.

The fourth requirement for Total Operations is that all links be aware of other links' continuous improvement efforts, both inside the organization and out. For example, when a major mouthwash manufacturer and a major retailer worked as a chain and not as independent links, sales of the mouthwash increased $8.5 million. The companies shared information throughout the chain to increase on-shelf availability, and this synthesis netted the increased sales. This success laid the foundation for an even more aggressive process of continuous improvement It also prevents the sacrifice of one link for the optimization of another and eliminates statements like, "The left hand doesn't know what the right hand is doing." Total Operations views all operational functions as a unit, and if one part of that unit is improved, then the rest must be also. So, Total Operations emphasizes continuous process improvement—just as SCS does.

The fifth Total Operations requirement involves people and attitude. People are what truly enable synthesis and their attitudes, more than any other single factor, drive the success of Total Operations. If everyone involved in Total Operations is committed to the goal of satisfying the ultimate customer, everyone wins.

Perhaps you have noticed a pattern here. If you have, then you are on the right track. The pattern is, simply, that Total Operations and SCS share similar goals with an ultimate destination—total integration. Both look at the whole through shared information and processes, and so both add value to the whole. However, they have different scopes. Although Total Operations can be applied to the supply chain, its main scope is an entire organization. In fact, on occasion I have recommended adopting Total Operations before adopting SCS. A Total Operations view prepares a company for SCS. In short, and in other words, SCS is a Total Operations concept.

10

SCS AND CUSTOMER SATISFACTION

"Customers only pay for what is of use to them and gives them value."

—Peter Drucker

The power in the marketplace has shifted from the producers to consumers. At one time, customers would hear, "You want that car in red by Friday? I'm sorry, but that's not possible. You can either purchase it in green here today or you can wait six weeks for another shipment of red cars to come in." Now they hear, "You want a blue shirt on Monday for $15? Absolutely. No problem. How else can I help?" Increasingly, end users are dictating the pace of Change. To quote an October 21, 1999, article from *Supply Chain Report*, "Companies that want to stay on the road to success must put customers in the driver's seat. For better or worse, consumer demand—not technology—will steer a thriving company's overall business strategy and determine what course a supply chain should take."

SCS recognizes how important customer satisfaction is for success and competitive advantage. Therefore, SCS emphasizes creating and maintaining close, good relationships with customers. When customers' thoughts, wants, and needs drive innovation and flow of goods and services from raw materials suppliers to retailers and ultimately back to those customers, you have customer satisfaction.

Customer satisfaction is not customer service. Customer service is a measurement of how well a company performs to an internally generated customer service requirement. For example, a few years ago, I was sent out of my way to the wrong gate by a major airline that claimed it had been ranked first in customer service each year from 1994 to 1997. I was informed by a ticket agent, "We usually do use this gate for Cincinnati, but not today. There is no way you can make it to gate C-32 in time." I was very unhappy. I was a customer of that airline and I was not at all satisfied. That's because that airline is not really interested in its customers or their satisfaction. What they are interested in is meeting and exceeding their measure of *customer service*, which is on-time arrivals. Their method for meeting this measure is to pad their schedules so that, even with a high level of incompetence, they can appear to be on time.

This is what I like to call "Customer Service Self-Centeredness," and it has nothing to do with satisfying the customer.

This chapter explains the difference between customer service and customer satisfaction, defines customer satisfaction, and explains why customer satisfaction is a core competency of SCS.

CUSTOMER SATISFACTION IS NOT CUSTOMER SERVICE

There is often a major disconnect between internally measured customer service results and actual customer satisfaction, as exhibited by that airline. This is common with Tompkins Associates clients, who measure their warehouse performance on order fill rates, on-time shipments, order picking accuracy, etc., while the customers measure their satisfaction based on the ease of doing business (e.g. with quality of information, consistency of receipt timing, and so on).

I'll use one of these clients as an example. One of the principals told me, when I asked how the client he was working for was doing on customer satisfaction, "Great."

"Super," I replied. "How do you know that?"

He answered, "Here's their chart on fill rate, here's their chart on backorders, here's their chart on on-time deliveries, here's their chart on damage, and here's their chart on complaints."
Every one of these charts was impressive. I then asked him if he had spoken with any of our client's customers. He said no, so we called several. Here is what we heard:

- "If there were anyone else that could fill the orders for the products we need, we'd go to them."
- "This company is not reliable."
- "We place an order but receive three shipments. These folks are clowns."
- "These people aren't doing good work."
- "I can't read their invoices. I don't have a clue what I'm supposed to be paying on this paperwork they send me."
- "I call their customer service and they put me on hold for an hour and a half and then make me talk to some stupid computer."

Another client had a similar story. The president told me the history of his firm and its many years of success. Then, he told me that the last two years of his company's history were years of stagnation, losses, and personal anguish. I began probing. After covering several topics, I finally asked, "How are you doing with customer satisfaction?"

He responded, "I can't explain why our customers are so unhappy with us; we are doing a super job on customer service."

I did some research and discovered the following:

1. Customer service was defined as orders being shipped as ordered two days after receipt, with an order fill rate above 90 percent.
2. The company was shipping the orders accurately 99.2 percent of the time, 99.4 percent of the time within two days, with an order fill rate of 99.7 percent (by lines).

3. Customer complaints were infrequent.
4. Although customer service was good, there was a feeling that customers were not happy. This feeling was caused by the fact that repeat orders were, for an unidentified reason, down.

The situation with both of these clients was an illness I mentioned at the beginning of this chapter—"Customer Service Self-Centeredness." This disease can slowly or quickly destroy companies, and can only be cured by a shift in thinking away from customer service and toward customer satisfaction.

THE VALUE OF CUSTOMER SATISFACTION—OPENSITE TECHNOLOGIES

OpenSite Technologies, located in Research Triangle Park, North Carolina, was the first development company to offer software solutions for online auction sites. Understanding that the needs of smaller organizations differ from those of large corporations, OpenSite provides three levels of functionality for its package so that clients do not purchase more than they need to being e-commerce transactions.

The inexpensive Professional edition offers style and template editors, digital certificate authentication, reserve pricing, and international user capability. The Merchant edition includes online storefront building and seller administration date, in addition to the functionality of the Professional edition. The Corporate edition, with the highest level of robust functionality, allows for analysis of data and private auction generation.

The recognition that e-commerce penetration is different for several tiers of clients has won OpenSite Technologies several awards for pioneering in its field.

WHAT IS CUSTOMER SATISFACTION?

Customer satisfaction is the output of logistics, SCM, and SCS. It is also a measure of the effectiveness of logistics, SCM, and SCS. It is the means by which companies attempt to differentiate their products, keep customers loyal, improve profits, and become the supplier of choice. In other words, it is an ongoing, escalating, value-added process of meeting requirements and exceeding expectations.

The difference between logistics, SCM, and SCS customer satisfaction is the level of customer satisfaction the customer registers for each. If a firm today adopts a logistics approach, it will have poor customer satisfaction. If it adopts an SCM perspective, it will typically have good satisfaction with the one downstream link but no real difference for the ultimate customer. Only SCS delivers true continuous improvement to the ultimate consumer as it is only in SCS that the whole chain is focused on the ultimate customer.

Customer satisfaction is a scientific process. Its formula was discussed in Chapter 2. It requires companies to divest themselves of their self-interests while fixating on the needs, expectations, and perceptions of those to whom they provide products and services. Supply chains must know and be able to identify the special needs of each level of their customer base. They must understand the customer tier.

THE CUSTOMER TIER

No company or supply chain has only one kind of customer. A customer base is made of people, and no two are alike. Each person has their own set of expectations, and each requires different services. Identifying the many different aspects of a company's customer base is vital. Such identification can be as broad and thorough as a company chooses, as long as one critical point drives it: Every customer is different and demands different levels of service.

For example, one of our clients, a grocery chain, and I were discussing customers. I asked, "Who are the customers, really?"

The reply was, "We've got lots of customers."

"But where do you make your money?" I persisted.

The client didn't know, so a market research firm was hired to do a study.

When the study was complete, the research showed that they had three kinds of customers: those that spent $20 a week in the store, those that spent about $75 a week, and those that spent $150 a week. Those that spent $20 a week cost the client $3 each time they visited the store; those that spent $75 a week earned the client $6 each time they visited the store; and those that spent $150 a week earned the client $30 each visit. In this case, then, there were three levels of service necessary. Unfortunately, the client did not understand that the customer level that brought in the most money should receive the best services. Instead, they created a special cashier for the customers spending only $20 a week while their best customers waited in longer lines.

People also change while they are an organization's or company's customers; therefore, companies cannot maintain customer satisfaction with the same set of services and value-adds that satisfied yesterday. As customers progress in their patronage, they will expect more and require more to be satisfied. Customer satisfaction, as a core competency of SCS, is a continuous improvement process. It is not a policy to implement; it is a process to be pursued continually.

Understanding the basic customer tier enables companies to pursue customer satisfaction in a highly focused and specialized manner. The tier is made up of three levels of customers with three corresponding levels of satisfaction. The first is the visitor level. "Visitors" are customers who occasionally purchase products and services but have no lasting commitment to the company. To them, satisfaction comes from the fundamental aspects of the product. These customers define satisfaction in terms of product features and cost.

The second level is the associates level. "Associates" are customers that regularly, but not exclusively, purchase a customer's products and services. Because the associates' experiences have grown since they started out as visitors, their expectations have also increased. As they become associates, they begin to take features and cost for granted, and turn their attention to quality. This is a serious challenge because quality is defined differently by different customers.

HOW CUSTOMER SATISFACTION AND THE CUSTOMER TIER WORK TOGETHER

Consider a situation in which a company produces an excellent product at a competitive cost with high quality, but little extra value added. Let's say the customer's perception of service was 100 points. If that customer is a visitor, whose expectation of service is only 40, then their customer satisfaction is high at a 60 (100-40=60). However, if that customer is an associate, who expected an excellent product, competitive cost, and high quality and therefore had a point value of 90, then their customer service is low at only 10 (100-90=10). Or, if that customer is a partner, who expected an excellent product, competitive cost, high quality, and considerable value-added support and had a 110-point expectation of service, then the level of customer satisfaction is -10 (100 − 110 = -10). This can be described as a customer dissatisfaction level of 10.

These examples explain why the president of the company with the long history was having difficulty. As customers' expectations increase from visitor to associate to partner, without a corresponding increase in the customers' perception of customer service received, then satisfaction quickly becomes dissatisfaction. The company thought that customer satisfaction would remain the same if they kept the same level of service or improved it slightly. This is a self-centered view of their offerings. They did not try to keep pace with their customers' increased expectations. This eventually will position a company for failure.

The third level is the partner's level. "Partners" are customers who have moved a company to the primary position on their lists in a product category. Through time and maintained satisfaction, they have come to the place where they always choose their preferred company first. Like associates, however, their expectations have grown and so have their requirements for satisfaction. They still expect features, cost, and quality, but they also require new value-added support like special handling, special delivery, extra services, training, and so on. SCS only applies to partners.

To maintain satisfaction while transforming visitors into partners, companies must know their customers well enough to evolve with them, and then be willing and able to make the evolution. They must keep in mind that SCS customer satisfaction grows out of link focus on the ultimate consumer and that all their customers must become partners if they are to achieve SCS. This will win continuous customer satisfaction.

THE ELEMENTS OF CUSTOMER SATISFACTION

Because customer satisfaction is a scientific process, it has specific elements that define it. These elements are grouped in three categories: pre-transaction, transaction, and post-transaction. The pre-transaction elements are as follows:

- Advises on non-availability
- Provides quality sales representation
- Monitors stock levels
- Consults on new product and package development
- Communicates target delivery dates
- Reviews product depth and breadth regularly.

The transaction elements are

- Ordering convenience
- Order acknowledgement
- Credit terms offered
- Handling of questions
- Frequency of delivery
- Order cycle time and reliability
- On-time deliveries

- Order status information
- Order tracking capabilities
- Fill rate percentage
- Shipment shortage
- Back order percentages
- Product substitutions
- Ability to handle emergency orders.

Post transaction elements are

- Invoice accuracy
- Returns and adjustments
- Well-stacked loads
- Easy-to-read packaging
- Quality of packaging.

If your chain offers these elements, then you are on the path to Customer Satisfaction. They indicate that the organization believes that de-massification of a product, rather than mass production, will be a driver of exemplary customer satisfaction. They allow the customer to be the co-creator of value, and they promote ongoing customer dialogue. They also indicate that the company believes that it is good business to treat customers as individuals rather than as demographics.

WHY CUSTOMER SATISFACTION IS A CORE COMPETENCY OF SCS

Consider the questions that must be answered to bring about high levels of customer satisfaction. They are

1. Who is the customer?
2. What does the customer want?
3. How do we increase customer satisfaction?

When customer satisfaction is the only concern, companies define and identify all sorts of customers, knowing that they must exceed the wants, needs, and expectations of all of them.

SCS also requires that we ask these questions. However, there is a difference in the customer satisfaction focus of SCS. It grows out of the focus of links on the ultimate customer until the entire chain focuses on the ultimate customer, or the end-user. SCS identifies the ultimate customer and what he or she wants, and then, by its very nature, increases customer satisfaction. This is because SCS allows everyone along the supply chain to adopt a culture for customer satisfaction based on a shared, consistent direction for the entire supply chain and an attitude of progressive, open, continuous improvement, and learning.

Now, consider a few of the specific steps for increasing customer satisfaction. They are

1. Reducing costs
2. Increasing quality
3. Promoting teamwork
4. Responding to customer needs.

If you take these steps, which are generally applied to a company, and apply them to the supply chain, then you have SCS. SCS reduces costs by simplifying the processes of manufacturing and distribution, reducing scrap and rework, and eliminating operations and delays. It increases quality because it encourages employees of every organization along the supply chain to go beyond "doing it right the first time" to "doing it better the next time." They establish standards and implement process control at all levels to achieve these standards, and allow the shipment of orders accurately without stockouts.

MEETING CUSTOMER NEEDS—THEORY OF POSTPONEMENT

Traditionally, manufacturing did all the work, and warehouses simply stored the product. Blurring the boundaries between manufacturing and warehousing until there are No Boundaries is what SCS is all about. By getting the value-added activities closer to the customer (i.e., doing them at the warehouse at the last moment before shipment), organizations can eliminate double handling of product, increase customer responsiveness, and add more value to SKUs throughout the pipeline.

Two types of postponement exist. One simply delays the customization of product. An apparel manufacturer might produce the same dress for seven different distributors.

Through cooperation of the supply chain partners, the warehouses receive the one dress, generic thus far, and place labels and tags on it as per the specific requirements of the customers. The manufacturer can concentrate on making the apparel and not tie up resources performing operations that the warehouses can do later on in the pipeline.

The second type of postponement is called merge-in-transit. This is a process used frequently in the computer industry. Components are received in the warehouse from various OEMs and CEMs: a keyboard from A, a CPU shell from B, a mouse from C, a hard drive from D, and so forth. Kitting and packing occurs at the warehouse based on customer specifications.

With postponement, manufacturers have less inventory to control, warehouses take an important role in the supply chain (rather than be perceived as a cost center, which is traditional), and customers receive what they want. Postponement operates with No Boundaries.

SCS promotes teamwork because everyone along the supply chain communicates the information necessary for gaining competitive advantage for that supply chain. After all, we are in a world that is increasingly defining competition as supply chain vs. supply chain rather than company vs. company. It responds to customer needs, because through SCS, cycle times are reduced, flexibility is increased, and customers in trouble receive the assistance they need.

In summary, SCS and customer satisfaction are irrevocably intertwined. You cannot have SCS without customer satisfaction and that is why it is a core competency of SCS.

11

SCS AND MANUFACTURING SYNTHESIS

"A great factory with the machinery all working and revolving with absolute and rhythmic regularity and with the men all driven by one impulse, and moving in unison as though a constituent part of the mighty machine, is one of the most inspiring examples of directed force that the world knows."

—Thomas Nelson Page

Suppose your circulatory system was not connected to your gastrointestinal system and both systems work quite well apart from each other. At first, this might seem to be a satisfactory arrangement. Your blood flows well and you are digesting your food with few ill effects. However, what would you do if you wanted toxins removed from your blood by your kidneys? You would have to connect the systems and hope for no leaks.

The poor connectivity between biological systems is the equivalent of boundaries between functions on the supply chain. These boundaries require manual connections, which, in turn, may cause leaks. In other words, they create problems that would not arise if they functioned as an organic whole with No Boundaries. This is particularly true for manufacturing, which functions much more efficiently and effectively when its processes are synthesized.

Now, imagine that someone comes along and tells you that your circulatory system is not necessary at all and you should remove it. How long do you think you would live? Interestingly, that's what SCM says about manufacturing. SCM often treats manufacturing as a peripheral player in the success of the supply chain. SCS, however, knows that without manufacturing, there would be no integration and no synthesis. As SKU customization and customer-ready product preparation become postponed to the last possible minute, traditional roles in manufacturing are becoming less of a means for securing competitive advantage. To remove the boundaries from manufacturing and merge these traditional roles, manufacturing synthesis is necessary.

Manufacturing synthesis is the combination of lean manufacturing, agile manufacturing, and Winning Manufacturing that incorporates cellular manufacturing. This chapter defines lean, agile, cellular, and Winning Manufacturing, explains manufacturing synthesis, and demonstrates why manufacturing synthesis is a core competency of SCS.

LEAN MANUFACTURING

Lean manufacturing, which is based on the Toyota Production System, is a series of flexible processes that allow the manufacture of products at lower cost. "Lean" is used to describe it because, when compared to mass production, it uses less of everything. It eliminates non-value-added waste in the production stream, and its theoretical objective is a lot size of one. A lean manufacturer is continuously improving in the direction of this theoretical objective.

The elements of lean manufacturing include
- Equipment reliability—equipment that runs when needed
- Process capability—processes that always produce quality
- Continuous flow—the material flows in small lots through production
- Error proofing—ways to prevent the product from being built wrong
- Stop-the-line quality system—if items of poor quality are appearing on the production line, the line is stopped
- Kanban system—a pull material flow system that pulls materials through the production process based on customer demand
- Visual management—when utilized fully, a new employee can understand how to do a job from the visual information in the plant and all employees understand the performance of the plant
- In-station process control—each workstation has the information and equipment for the worker to inspect and produce good quality parts
- Quick changeover—a system to change from one product to another quickly
- Takt Time—production is paced to customer demand. Takt Time equals the time available to produce a product divided by the number of parts that the customer wants to buy.

These elements all help eliminate waste, and cutting waste is the foundation of lean manufacturing. Waste is defined as "anything that consumes material or labor and that does not add value to the final end product that is received or purchased by the end customer."

Implementation of lean manufacturing is often referred to as de-massification and can create the following results:
- Reduction in inventory
- Increased productivity
- Reduction in the floor space required to make a product
- Reduction in scrap and rework
- Reduced lead time
- Reduced changeover time.

THE VALUE OF LEAN MANUFACTURING—GENERAL MOTORS

In 1998, General Motors opened a plant in Gilwice, Poland, that represented a leaner manufacturing future for the automobile manufacturer. With a price tag of $300 million, this plant is only 800,000 square feet and is more flexible than the monoliths of GM's past. Its smaller size does not represent a proportionate reduction in output. On the contrary, the plant produces 150,000 cars yearly, compared with 215,000 cars in the 3-million-square-foot Shreveport, Louisiana facility, and 244,000 cars in the 4.1-million-square-foot Spring Hill, Tennessee Saturn plant.

Standard storage was reduced from a typical measurement of 350,000 square feet to 140,000 square feet, and only 20 percent of the body shop was automated. GM saved money in many ways, as well. The Gilwice plant produces several kinds of cars rather than just one like the Bowling Green, Kentucky plant which only produces Corvettes (32,000 a year in one million square feet). The Gilwice plant also employs a workforce eager and willing to learn multiple tasks. The line employees are encouraged to learn and master ten jobs in two minutes each. Cross-functional training has paid off; there is no employee in the Gilwice plant who is unable to take on another function in peak or crisis periods.

What has this done for GM? The plant's effort to create flexibility in its inventory management, its production methods, and its staff has enabled GM to save money in many ways. Thinking out of the box is not typically associated with the automotive industry; however, GM's ability to get past the traditions of its vertical (huge plants, employees with narrowly defined job functions) is an example of Winning Manufacturing.

AGILE MANUFACTURING

Agile manufacturing is one step beyond lean manufacturing. Agile manufacturing was developed as a response to a number of issues:

- Fast and unpredictable turbulence in the marketplace
- The demand for high quality, low volume, and short product life cycles
- The decline of mass production
- Customer satisfaction
- Demands for high levels of value-added services
- Products that are rich in information
- A focus on people and relationships.

The characteristics of agile manufacturing include

- Customer enrichment
- Competitiveness through cooperation
- Organizational focus on change and uncertainty
- A highly educated and empowered workforce
- Emphasis on the customer as an individual
- Relationship-driven partnerships
- Flexible management structures
- Virtual corporations
- Products and services rich in information
- Integration and flexibility.

Agile manufacturing has four underlying principles: delivering value to the customer, being ready for change, valuing human knowledge and skills, and forming virtual partnerships. Two critical elements of agile manufacturing are flexibility and modularity. To review what was discussed in Chapter 3, flexibility means a variety of items can be manufactured with little or no change in procedure or methodology. Modularity means that manufacturing is capable of producing different volumes of items with little or no change in procedure or methodology.

THE VALUE OF MODULARITY—BAYER DIAGNOSTICS

Bayer Diagnostics's ADVIA is the first multi-functional sampling workstation that does not require blood test batching. Until ADVIA was offered, anemic patient management meant using two machines for two different blood tests, which was staff and setup intensive. ADVIA provides hospitals and clinics more versatility in their phlebotomy operations as well as more efficiency. Daily maintenance is automated, less space is necessary, cross-training employees is easier, and one entire workstation has been eliminated.

CELLULAR MANUFACTURING

Cellular manufacturing helps companies reduce WIP and respond to change more quickly, both of which are goals of manufacturing synthesis. In cellular manufacturing, Group Technology principles are used to design efficient cells. Each of these cells is focused on producing "families" of parts. Process sequences maximize the layout, resulting in smaller batch quantities that run through the cell with little material handling and small WIP inventories. In other words, the parts continually flow through the cell in process sequence, from start to finish without ever leaving the cell. Typically, companies considering cellular manufacturing produce a wide variety of complex but similar parts.

WINNING MANUFACTURING

Winning Manufacturing is a step beyond lean, agile, and cellular manufacturing, although it utilizes all three. Winning Manufacturing is a never-ending journey of continuous improvement. It addresses everything from product development to inventories to marketing. Companies that adopt Winning Manufacturing produce quality products, have satisfied customers, identify manufacturing as a strategic strength, are profitable, and grow.

Winning Manufacturing embodies a philosophy of dynamic consistency. Pursuing Winning Manufacturing requires complying with these two critical qualities:

1. It is a continuous process of "improve, improve, improve."

2. It is anchored on a full, integrating understanding of 20 Requirements of Success (see Appendix A). All 20 of these Requirements of Success must be embraced.

The Winning Manufacturing path of success and the Winning Manufacturing process are illustrated in Figures 11.1 and 11.2. They are also discussed in detail in my book, *Winning Manufacturing*, and will be further pursued in my upcoming book, *The Future Capable Company*.

FIGURE 11.1: THE WINNING MANUFACTURING PATH OF SUCCESS

Each cycle of the Winning Manufacturing process begins with three distinct tasks: understanding the 20 Requirements of Success, understanding external issues, and understanding internal issues. The understanding of external and internal issues is also of critical importance in SCS, so I want to discuss them briefly here.

Understanding external issues demands an awareness of factors outside a company that affect it. These factors include shifts in the marketplace, availability of new technology, actions taken by competitors, and government regulations. If a company does not stay aware of external factors, it will become self-centered and

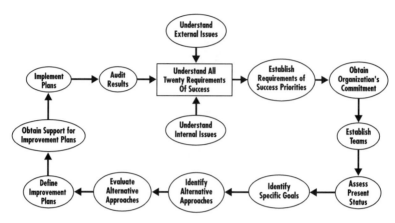

FIGURE 11.2: THE WINNING MANUFACTURING PROCESS

lose touch with reality. Once this happens, organizations have difficulty establishing priorities. They may begin doing the wrong things and doing them efficiently.

Understanding internal issues requires awareness of a company's business plan. Manufacturing management should be intimately involved in the business planning for a company. The priorities for Winning Manufacturing should be established within the context of the company's business plan. Winning Manufacturing cannot be achieved if it is not part of the overall business plan.

MANUFACTURING SYNTHESIS

Manufacturing synthesis can be summarized in two words: continuous flow. Continuous flow means balancing a series of operations for reduced production lot sizes to create a continuous, controlled indexing of parts through production.

Manufacturing synthesis can be accomplished by
1. Reducing lead times significantly
2. Reducing production lot sizes and setup times
3. Minimizing all uncertainty and increasing discipline
4. Balancing all manufacturing operations
5. Implementing a straightforward and transparent production and inventory control system
6. Reducing inventories drastically.

The sections that follow will discuss these elements more fully.

CUSTOMER LEAD TIMES

There are three types of lead times: manufacturing lead time, production lead time, and customer lead time. Manufacturing lead time is that time from material availability at the first manufacturing operation until the last manufacturing operation is complete. Production lead time is that time from the ordering of all materials for items production until the last manufacturing operation is complete. Customer lead time is that time between customer ordering and customer receipt. Manufacturing synthesis requires the reduction of customer lead times significantly. This depends on the historical approach to lead time and the amount of product customization. The less attention that has been focused on lead time, the greater the opportunity for lead time reduction.

To reduce customer lead times significantly, the methodology for doing business must change. The procedures to be followed are as follows:

1. Document present customer lead time—this document should be a flow chart with the times recorded for each activity. It should accurately document actual occurrences, not standard operating procedures.

2. Competitive analysis—know your competitors' customer lead times. The more you know about what your competitors are doing, the better prepared you will be to compete with them.

3. Leadership must establish a goal—this goal should include the commitment to reducing customer lead times by doing the analysis and by rethinking the methods of doing business. Therefore, the goal should be more detailed than a statement that says "Let's cut customer lead time from five weeks to three days."

4. Identify bottlenecks—the flow chart created in Step 1 should be used as the starting point for identifying bottlenecks. On this flow chart, the goals for each activity should be recorded and the sum of the goals for each activity should surpass the reduction required to achieve the goal. For example, if the goal is to reduce customer lead time to three days, then the sum of the goals for each activity should be two or two and one-half days.

5. Create multi-department teams—these teams should be broad-based and comprised of individuals who focus on specific sets of activities. They should also be given the authority to change business methods to achieve the lead-time goals. They should also emphasize simplification, embrace teamwork, and eliminate uncertainty.

Short customer lead times make it possible to plan and control priorities; thus, reducing customer lead times will create lower inventories, quicker customer response, improved employee satisfaction, improved quality, and reduced manufacturing costs. Customers will benefit from receiving their orders quickly, and that increases market share. Employees will be more satisfied because they will be working for a responsive, successful company. Even quality will improve.

PRODUCTION LOT SIZES

Reducing production lot sizes, which is facilitated by reducing setup times, shortens manufacturing lead times. You can reduce production lot sizes as follows:

1. Document present lot sizes.
2. Identify specific lot sizes for reduction.
3. Reduce setup times by following the Toyota Motor Company concepts and techniques (see below).
4. Calculate the economic lot size (where setup cost equals the inventory carrying cost).
5. Identify alternative methods for handling the economic lot size between operations.
6. Evaluate alternative methods for efficient material handling.
7. Justify the investment required to reduce setup times and to handle materials efficiently, with the savings resulting from the reduction in lot size.
8. Define and obtain support for specific improvement plants.
9. Implement the reduced setup time and the material handling equipment as justified and begin production of reduced lot sizes.

The concepts developed by the Toyota Motor Company to reduce setup are

1. Separate the internal setup (setup activities that must occur inside a machine and require that it not be in operation) from the external setup (setup activities that occur external to the machine and can take place while the machine is in operation). Assure that all external setup operations are complete before the machine is taken out of production. Only internal setup activities should be performed when the machine is out of operation.

2. Convert as much of the internal setup as possible to external setup. By altering the machine or the setup activities, the total setup time can be minimized.

3. Eliminate the adjustment process. By altering the machines or the setup, a standard or automatic setting can be established that eliminates the need for adjustment.

4. Abolish the setup. Standardizing parts can lead to an elimination of setup. Another approach is to have parallel operations performing different operations and, by switching a mechanism, using only the operations that apply to each product.

To apply these concepts, you should standardize the external setup actions and the machines, use quick fasteners, use a supplementary tool, consider multi-person setup crews, and automate the setup process. Reducing setup times makes a reality of high-variety, high-productivity, low-inventory, and small production lot size manufacturing. This is manufacturing synthesis.

UNCERTAINTY

Minimizing uncertainty must begin with a definition of events that have caused surprises, crises, or changes in plans. This can be done by surveying a cross section of manufacturing personnel to obtain an initial list of target events followed by an ongoing activity whereby manufacturing personnel record events that result in surprises, crises, or changes in plan. Figure 11.3 is an example of the procedure to be followed for each target event.

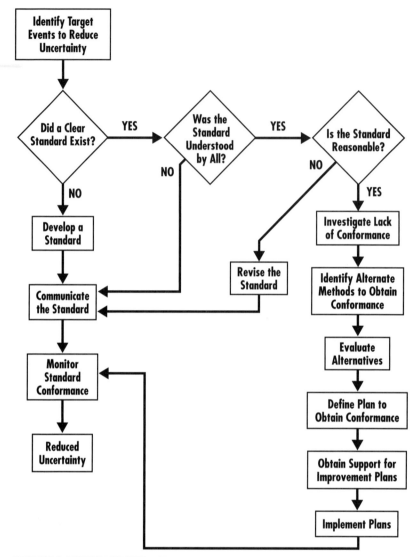

FIGURE 11.3: REDUCING UNCERTAINTY

Minimizing uncertainty also means creating standards and establishing discipline. A standard of performance must be established, accepted, and followed. Everyone involved must understand and respond to the following standards:

- Product quality
- Delivery schedule
- Delivery quantity
- Process performance

- Process duration
- Machine downtime
- Setup duration
- Production methodology
- Part tolerances
- Product packaging.

Discipline is the resolution to embrace a standard and not accept anything other than performance at or above the standard. This discipline must be uncompromising and applied uniformly throughout a company. There can be no exceptions. All vendors, organizational elements, and production operations must have this level of discipline.

Minimizing uncertainty will bring quiet, order, and stability to manufacturing so that harmony and continuity will exist in an error-free, disruption-free, crisis-free environment. Events that impair manufacturing, such as sloppy product development schedules, quality problems, maintenance problems, unreliable employees, and untimely vendor shipments, are no longer part of the manufacturing process. This allows the continuous flow that is so critical to manufacturing synthesis.

BALANCE

Balanced manufacturing operations require continuous flow (already defined), focused departments, sequential flow, and standardization. "Focused departments" means that all operations required to produce a family of parts are located in a focused area. "Sequential flow" means the unchanged flow of parts through a series of operations. Standardization requires determining the cycle time, elemental time, standard operations routine, standard quality of WIP, and the standard of performance. The starting point is determining the cycle time that must be met to satisfy production requirements.

The first step in achieving balanced manufacturing is to document present WIP inventory because it is a symptom of unbalanced operations. Once the levels of WIP inventory have been documented, the following questions need to be addressed:

1. Have setup time reductions been implemented? What is the potential for setup time reductions?

2. Have production lot sizes been reduced? What is the potential for production lot size reductions?

3. Has uncertainty been minimized? What potential exists for minimization of uncertainty?

4. Have focused departments and focused factories been implemented? What opportunities exist for the creation of focused departments and focused factories?

5. Do production lots continuously flow through manufacturing operations? Are all WIP inventory buffers justifiable? Are WIP inventory buffers high-turnover, low-inventory hesitations in the continuous flow of materials?

6. Have the proper procedures been put in place to maximize sequential flow? How can WIP inventory be reduced by implementing sequential flow?

7. Have standards of performance been established, accepted, and followed for each operation, focused department, and focused factory? How can the standards of performance be more rigorously pursued?

8. Have the operational costs of just-in-time been analyzed? Is there a proper understanding of the tradeoff between operating costs and balance?

9. Have capacity bottlenecks been properly analyzed? Has the issue of balance been properly addressed both before and after the capacity bottleneck?

10. If not already answered, why does WIP inventory exist? Are all WIP inventories justifiable?

No manufacturing operation will ever achieve total balance. Instead, your objective should be to achieve greater balance, not perfect balance. Answering the questions above will allow you to prioritize opportunities; identify and evaluate alternatives; and define, approve, and implement improvement plans. Combining these activities with continuous improvement will lead to greater and greater balance.

PRODUCTION AND INVENTORY CONTROL

The key elements of a successful, manufacturing synthesis production and inventory control system are

1. A production and inventory control system that is a part

of the Winning Manufacturing process. This is radically different from traditional production and inventory control. Production planning is more predictable because manufacturing and marketing work as a team, and product families will be produced at a much more uniform rate. Product development is an integrated, iterative process with more standard components. Continuous flow manufacturing is the norm. Production schedules are met because uncertainty is reduced and balance is greater.

2. A production and inventory control system that is straightforward and transparent. Production and inventory are controlled by defining the products, families, and options to be produced; defining the volume of products, families, and options to be produced; specifying a production plan; defining when materials and capacity should be present to meet the production plan; scheduling material delivery from vendors and focused factories; and monitoring schedule adherence.

3. A production and inventory control system that is Theory of Constraints (TOC)-based. TOC is a management philosophy. It is based on the key premise that only a few work centers control the output of an entire factory for each product line and that managing these capacity constraining resources (CCRs), or bottlenecks, maximizes the output of the factory. TOC utilizes the drum-buffer-rope method to schedule the flow of materials with an eye to market demand and inventory and operating expense reductions. The drum, or constraint, sets the pace of the system; the buffer is the protective window of time that ensures that the drum never runs dry; and the rope is the schedule that releases materials in a synchronous manner that assures smooth material flow. By determining the performance limits for all production processes (i.e., recognizing bottlenecks), organizations utilizing the TOC methodology can see the following results: improved quality and increased throughput.

The results of these elements are vendor and focused department schedules. Adherence to these schedules results in production and inventory control.

INVENTORIES

Reducing inventories begins with the documentation of present levels of inventory. These levels should then be compared to whatever industry benchmarks are available. Factors to consider in determining the levels of inventory include industry norms, production constraints, seasonality, customer requirements, material availability, and production stability. After these factors have been considered, specific inventory reduction goals should be established. An inventory reduction team should then conduct an audit to determine why the present levels of inventory exist; this audit should also factor in the 20 Winning Manufacturing Requirements of Success. While considering the goal, the audit, the Requirements of Success, and the cost tradeoffs, specific recommendations to reduce inventory may be established and implemented by the team.

Reducing inventories allows organizations to focus on the problems that originally created the need for them. Full attention can be given to them because excessive inventories do not exist in manufacturing synthesis and, therefore, problems can be identified and solutions found quickly. Eliminating inventories makes it easier to maintain little or no inventory, which creates continuous flow, which leads to manufacturing synthesis.

WHY MANUFACTURING SYNTHESIS IS A CORE COMPETENCY OF SCS

Manufacturing synthesis focuses on the fact that long lead times make it impossible to plan and control priorities. Shorter lead times clear the shop floor of WIP inventory, conflicting manufacturing priorities, and other manufacturing problems. The results are reduced inventories, quicker customer response, higher levels of employee satisfaction, higher quality products, and lower manufacturing costs.

When the requirements of manufacturing synthesis are applied to the supply chain, the result is SCS manufacturing. SCS manufacturing is streamlined, straightforward, responsive, flexible, modular, and continuously improving. It responds to Change and Integration quickly and easily because of these characteristics. It is a time-based competitive approach to BTO that integrates both internal and external manufacturing resources to maximize customer satisfaction. It also allows customization, which often is a result of or a companion of BTO.

In summary, the result of applying manufacturing synthesis to the total supply chain is SCS manufacturing. Therefore, an organization that has successfully applied manufacturing synthesis in its internal operations can use the same methodology for applying it across the supply chain. This is why manufacturing synthesis is a core competency of SCS.

12

SCS AND DISTRIBUTION SYNTHESIS

"Efficiency is not enough. Agility is the key."
—Cranfield School of Management

In SCS, all distribution functions must work as one, with each distribution function being equally aware of other functions. In other words, SCS requires an integrated approach to distribution, which is distribution synthesis. As I stated in Chapter 9, distribution synthesis is making sure that the right manufacturing operations and right distribution centers (DCs) are in the right locations, holding the right amount of inventory, and that the right transportation is being used to fulfill the order to the satisfaction of the customer. When this is done from a link's perspective, it is called logistics. When it is done from a chain's perspective, the results are reduced inventory investments, reduced costs of distribution, improved customer satisfaction, and a streamlined flow of goods to the marketplace. This No Boundaries approach is SCS.

FLOW OF GOODS—DEFINING THE METATYPES

Understanding Flow of Goods (FOG) means understanding the physical and information flows necessary to support a specific supply chain process. FOG processes can be segmented in a number of ways and they are not mutually exclusive. The most common of these processes are

- DC/Warehouse Process—the customer order cycle and replenishment order cycle are physically independent but happen concurrently. APSs and ERPs are used to get them to work in unison. A further refinement is classifying the DCs by the level of control they wish to have on inventory, equipment, and labor.
- Supplier Hub Process—this process is similar to the DC/Warehouse process but has two additional attributes: ownership and invoicing. Ownership is retained by the vendor(s) for whom the facility is operated. Automatic invoicing is triggered by the supplier hub's WMS to the customer(s), as is title transfer.
- International Pre-Distribution Process—uses a product consolidation point of origin along with management of retail store order quantities to create full pallets and/or full container loads. The destination is either a specific store or even departments within the store.
- Rapid Development Logistics Process—used for one-time, high-volume supply chain efforts. An example is the number of efforts required each time Disney does a tie-in with McDonalds for a new movie. Overnight, in exact timing with the movie's release, thousands of McDonalds stores must receive the tie-in merchandise (action figures, cups, etc.).

■ Work Order Management Process—refers to processes where the logistics provider performs an additional set of operations on the product(s) before delivery to the end customer.

■ Direct to Customer Process—involves running a DC that ships, usually through parcel services, directly to the end customer.

—Ray Hood, President & CEO, EXE Technologies, Inc.

Distribution synthesis requires blurring boundaries between warehousing and transportation until there are No Boundaries, using a hybrid push/pull system that adjusts to more demanding customer satisfaction requirements. A foundation for achieving distribution synthesis is a Distribution Strategic Master Plan (DSMP). This chapter explains the process of a DSMP, explains third-party logistics, compares push and pull systems and hybrid push/pull systems, and describes why distribution synthesis is a core competency of SCS.

DISTRIBUTION STRATEGIC MASTER PLAN

Strategic planning is the process of deciding on the objectives of the firm, changes in the objectives, resources to attain these objectives, and policies to govern the acquisition use and disposition of resources. The objective of distribution strategic planning is to define the overall approach to stocking points, transportation, inventory management, customer satisfaction, and information systems and the way they relate in order to provide the maximum return on investment. A distribution strategic master plan (DSMP), therefore, features a strategic distribution network plan, a strategic warehouse plan, and a strategic transportation plan.

FACTORS INFLUENCING THE DSMP

Since distribution is a dynamic environment, business issues such as the global marketplace, the level of government involvement, the environment, and the issue of energy challenge it. At the same time, the customer requirements of increased pace, variety, and adaptability while reducing costs must be understood. Of course, these issues impact the internal pressures of distribution requirements to centralize, utilize third parties, improve information systems, increase productivity, and more fully utilize people.

Strategic planning is an offensive tool designed to guard against a predictable change in requirements, the timing of which can be anticipated. Strategic planning is directed at forecasting future needs far enough in advance of the actual requirements to allow enough lead time to efficiently meet those needs. Granted, forecasting with a long planning horizon is a risky business, and distribution plans based on such forecasts often prove unworkable. Nevertheless, the forecast is the best available information concerning the future, and it is foolish not to use that information to one's advantage.

The only way to survive the rapidly changing distribution environment today is to have good strategic plans that address the future needs of distribution and the factors influencing distribution. These factors are

- **Global Marketplace**—in today's world there is no choice but to understand the global strategy implications on all distribution decisions. As shifts occur in the world's trading patterns, this changes the distribution requirements, alters the location and number of warehouses, increases supply chain inventories, and creates new transportation opportunities and problems.
- **Government Involvement**—a global trend is for governments to deregulate many activities, most notably transportation. It is important to understand that, just as government involvement has an impact on distribution, distribution leadership has an obligation to have an impact on government on behalf of distribution.
- **Reverse Distribution**—an issue that is closely tied to the issue of government involvement is the issue of

reverse distribution. Reverse distribution has two aspects. One is returned goods—the returning a product back up the supply chain. The second is the task of recovering packaging and shipping materials and backhauling them to a central collection point for recycling. Handling the mechanics of reverse distribution requires significant attention. The issue of reverse logistics appears in a sidebar highlighting Pallet Management Systems in Chapter 13.

■ **Off-Highway Vehicles**—the EPA is pushing to regulate off-highway vehicles; this effort will include lift trucks and will further push warehouses in the direction of electric vehicles. The internal combustion lift trucks that will be sold in the future will need to meet much stricter emission standards, but in many applications, these vehicles will be replaced by electric vehicles.

■ **Energy**—the cost of energy is a major concern to transportation companies. In the United States, 60 percent of all energy consumption is for transportation. Although these costs tend to be buried in the overall cost of transportation, any significant shift in the cost of energy could have an impact on the costs of transportation and therefore on distribution. It is therefore important that, at least as a sensitivity issue, the issue of energy costs be viewed in making all distribution decisions.

■ **Pace**—there exists an accelerating rate of change in all aspects of human endeavor—social, political, economic, technological, ecological, and psychological. It is not surprising, then, that the reduction of lead times, shorter product lives, and increases in inventory turnover are resulting in significant increases in the pace of change in distribution. Distribution must be more responsive because of the demands being placed upon them by customers.

■ **Variety**—the variety of tasks handled by distribution will continue to increase. Special packaging, unitizing, pricing, labeling, kitting, and delivery requirements is becoming the norm. Distribution must perform operations that traditionally have been viewed as manufacturing operations. Systems and procedures will be put in place to handle information consistent with the desires of the customers.

- **Flexibility**—the most important aspect of flexible distribution is *versatility*—in equipment, systems, and workers. The design, specification, and implementation of versatile equipment is required to achieve flexible distribution. Warehouse storage rack and material handling equipment as well as transportation equipment should be selected with sufficient versatility to handle today's distribution requirements and, when justifiable, future requirements. Similarly, versatile systems have an impact of adapting customer labeling, automatic identification, communications, and documentation requirements. We never want to find ourselves saying to a customer, "I am sorry, our system does not allow us to accommodate your request." Lastly, we must have multi-skilled personnel to achieve flexible distribution. Overly restrictive work rules, excessive job classifications and labor grades, and insufficient training have often resulted in a lack of flexibility in distribution. Multi-skilling eliminates barriers between tasks, and workers better understand the implications of their performance.
- **Modularity**—the three most important aspects of modular distribution are modular distribution assets, modular work assignments, and time modularity. The issue of modular distribution assets has to do with the expansion and contraction of warehouse space and the increase or decrease of transportation equipment. Similarly, for transportation equipment, purchase and lease decisions as well as contract terms should be evaluated while considering both the long-term and short-term fluctuations in traffic. The challenge of modular work assignments has to do with the daily balance of work within a warehouse. Once people have been given multiple skills, it is important to be certain that people are assigned in such a way to allow for a continuous flow of materials through distribution. Lastly, to provide modular distribution is the issue of time modularity. Creativity in employee work

schedules can have a significant impact on an operation's output. Many distribution operations have been significantly improved by adjusting work schedules so that there is a balance between the staff on hand and the tasks to be performed. Not addressing the issue of time modularity often results in distribution operations having very low productivity.

■ **Price**—a prerequisite for the success of free enterprise is efficient, effective, and low cost distribution. Although the cost of distribution is less than 10 percent of the price the customer must pay, it is of the utmost importance to the customer that even this price be reduced. As a percentage of Gross National Product, distribution costs are down from a high of almost 15 percent to 11 percent and as a percentage of Gross Domestic Product, they are down from a high of almost 18 percent to below 12 percent. Thus, it is very important that the cost of distribution even be further reduced.

■ **Centralization**—fewer and larger centralized warehouses are replacing the greater in number, smaller, decentralized warehouses of the past. There will be fewer managers and administrative people involved with distribution as integrated distribution is pursued and distribution staffs are centralized. Along with the centralization of warehouses and staffs comes the centralization of order entry, customer service, and data processing. The increased responsiveness of transportation at lower costs, the focus on the total cost of distribution, the realities of customer satisfaction, pace, variety, and adaptability all are pointed toward the centralization theme. The trend toward centralized distribution will result in higher inventory turnover, which will, in turn, lead to new opportunities for automation and sophisticated information systems.

■ **Third Party Logistics**—third party logistics (3PL) is the utilization of an outside firm to perform some or all of the distribution functions presently performed internally. As companies better understand integrated distribution and as distribution leadership better understands the costs of distribution, there will be an increasing trend toward the outsourcing of portions of the distribution function.

- **Information Systems**—information technology is impacting everything from business to education to entertainment. It is not surprising, therefore, that information technology is having, and will continue to have, a major impact on distribution. It has become clear that all distribution documentation must be electronic. All distribution paperwork needs to be scrutinized and eliminated whenever possible. It is important to realize that paperwork means delays, errors, additional work and, therefore, wasted time and money. Distribution information systems must be real-time and paperless and standardized throughout the distribution supply chain.

- **Productivity**—accountability for performance in distribution must be increased, which means establishing standards, identifying opportunities for improvement, measuring performance, and taking action to assure continuous distribution improvement. Most importantly, productivity must increase. Maintaining the status quo is totally unacceptable.

- **People**—customers drive the business of distribution, but performance depends upon distribution people. Customer satisfaction results from contact with distribution people and so an important, ongoing distribution issue remains in people. In the past, distribution workers were narrowly focused, having a specialized skill or technical strength. The people needed in distribution today must adopt a broader view of distribution, a more integrated understanding of distribution, a team-based, participatory organizational culture, and a total dedication to the supply chain and to customer satisfaction.

STRATEGIC DISTRIBUTION NETWORK PLAN

The first step of the DSMP is a strategic distribution network plan. A good strategic distribution network plan will determine the network that can best provide the customer with the right goods, in the right quantity, at the right place, at the right time, while minimizing the total distribution costs.

The objective of strategic distribution network planning is to determine a plan that indicates the most economical way to ship and receive product while maintaining or increasing customer satisfaction. Strategic distribution network planning typically answers the following:

1. How many DCs should exist?
2. Where should the DC(s) be located?
3. How much inventory should be stocked at each DC?
4. What customers should be serviced by each DC?
5. How should the customers order from the DC?
6. How should the DCs order from vendors?
7. How frequently should shipments be made to each customer?
8. What should the satisfaction levels be?
9. What transportation methods should be utilized?

Strategic distribution network planning also considers future distribution requirements. To document the future distribution network requirements, it is not only important to understand the factors influencing distribution but also to understand the marketing strategies and sales forecast. The following list identifies questions that should be answered by marketing and sales:

- Are there any new products being developed? From where are they sourced? What is the target market area (geographically)?
- What are the ordering parameters right now? For example, what is the minimum order size? Are they changing any terms of order (e.g., charging for expedite service)?
- What is the direction of the market? (Packaging changes, wholesalers, mass merchants having more volume).
- Are sales increasing each year?
- Are customer shifts becoming apparent? Are fewer customers handling more volume?
- Have geographic shifts emerged? Have sales increased by geographic regions?

Planning a distribution network is a sequential process that continually needs updating. The steps taken in distribution design are listed below:

1. Document Distribution Network
2. Identify Delivery Requirements
3. Establish Database
4. Develop Alternative Networks
5. Model Annual Operating Costs
6. Evaluate Alternatives
7. Specify the Plan.

Some companies run into the pitfall of performing steps 3 through 6 before collecting and understanding the most important steps, which are 1 and 2. The answer to distribution network planning is only as good as the data put into the analysis. The following sections address the steps for strategic distribution network planning.

The steps for documenting the distribution network, identifying delivery requirements, and establishing the database can be done simultaneously. The main goal of these steps is to gain an understanding of the current system and define the requirements of the future system. To document the existing systems, information must be collected on the DCs and the transportation system. In gathering information on the DCs, it is critical to collect from all existing sites considered since the study could result in making recommendations on closing, moving or expanding the facilities. The following information needs to be collected for each site:

- Space Utilization—determine the utilization of the DC. This will allow you to determine the amount of physical inventory space that will be required if this facility is to be closed when the analysis is complete. It also identifies how much more inventory can be combined into this location.
- Layout and Equipment—list the equipment and layout of each facility. If you have a list of equipment available it will be easier to determine the investment requirements of a new or expanded facility.
- Warehouse Operating Procedures—understand the order picking and shipping procedures. If there are two

product lines in one location, are they picked and shipped together? Understand the differences in operating methods between facilities. This may tell why one facility achieves a higher throughput efficiency per person. Understand how replenishment orders are placed or pushed to the DC.

- Staffing Levels—document levels by position. Understand which jobs could be consolidated. Collect labor rates by level including fringe benefits.
- Receiving and Shipping Volumes—understand the number of incoming and outgoing trucks and the number of docks. This will be important if the facility is required to increase throughput.
- Building Characteristics—collect building characteristics such as clear height, lighting levels, column spacing, etc. Collect this for the same reason as layout information, but keep in mind to review expansion capabilities.
- Access to Location—review the access to main highways. Determine if this will have an effect on freight cost.
- Annual Operating Cost: Collect lease cost, taxes, insurance, maintenance, energy cost and other facility cost.
- Inventory—collect information on inventory turns and levels, fill rates, safety stock levels and ABC analysis. By having this information the savings of consolidating facilities can be determined. Also collect which and how much stock is slow moving or seasonal to help determine if it should be centralized in one location or if public warehouse space should be used. Get future inventory goals.
- Performance Reporting—understand the performance measures for satisfaction requirements, order completeness, shipping accuracy, etc.
- Freight Classes and Discounts—collect the freight classes and rates used. In addition to freight classes, get the discounts by carrier or location. It is also important to understand where the discounts apply (under which parameters, i.e., routes, minimum weights).
- Transportation Operating Procedures—understand how a certain mode of transport is selected and how a carrier is selected.

- Delivery Requirements—what are the delivery requirements (days of delivery) to the customer in days, and how is carrier performance measured? Is order completeness measured?
- Replenishment Weight/Cube—at what weight is a trailer cubed out? Get this information from each replenishment point and for a typical load of general merchandise.

One of the key data requirements in analyzing a distribution network is that of the delivery requirements (time order placement to receipt of the shipment). Therefore, the second step of a strategic distribution network plan is to identify the delivery requirements. If the requirements are not identifiable, a customer satisfaction gap analysis must be undertaken. The gap analysis is a series of questions directed at internal staff and customers. The purpose is to identify discrepancies between customer perception of satisfaction and satisfaction requirements. The key is to find the best service that maximizes profits.

The third step, establishing a database of orders that are to be modeled, can be accomplished while the existing network is being documented. This information should include ship-to locations, weight of the shipments, products ordered, and the quantity ordered. Once the data is established, the next step should be to validate the data. To ensure that the information was transferred properly, print out a few records of invoices and compare these to hard copies. Also, it is a good idea to prepare a summary report (sales, cases sold, weight shipped) for a sanity check to ensure all the data in the files was transferred. Once the data is valid, various analyses such as ABC analysis by picks, location (geographical), volumes, and product volumes by regions of the country should be run. These reports should be used to help determine alternatives.

Once the data has been collected, the next step consists of developing alternative networks. The input used to determine alternatives consists of site visits, future requirements, database analysis, and customer satisfaction surveys. Consideration must also be given to operating methods, as well as to criteria such as consolidating vendor shipments, centralizing slow moving items in one place, keeping company divisions separate, and direct shipment by vendors. Once alternative networks are determined, data must be collected on freight rates, warehouse cost, and labor cost for the alternative sites.

Various techniques for the fifth step, modeling annual operating costs, are available. The overall approach should closely resemble the following procedures:

1. Validate the existing network. Run a computer model to simulate the existing cost. Compare this cost to actual cost.

2. Run alternative networks. Once the model is valid, alternative networks should be run for present volumes and forecasted volumes.

3. Summarize runs and rank. Create a table to summarize cost by alternative. The table should list DC cost individually.

4. Summarize all annual costs and service factors. Create a table that indicates by alternative all the cost and service factors.

5. Perform a Sensitivity Analysis. Sensitivity analysis is based on the idea of setting up runs that fluctuate some components of the data. This could be a cost that is uncertain or one that might change. By modifying this single parameter, the effect on the run can be determined.

6. Determine all investment costs associated with each alternative. This includes the cost of new warehouse equipment required to save space, expansion, and construction cost, or any building modifications such as adding dock doors. This information will be of use in the next step.

The sixth step, evaluate alternatives, involves an economic analysis that compares the recommended network plan to the implementation cost. To do this analysis, you must determine all the investments and savings associated with each alternative. Costs such as new warehouse equipment, construction cost, or any building modification should be included. Additionally, the following information must be identified: personnel relocation, severance, stock relocation, computer relocation, taxes, equipment relocation, and the sale of existing land and buildings. The result of this step should be a return on investment of each alternative compared to the baseline.

Once this step is completed, a sensitivity analysis that fluctuates various costs and savings to see which alternatives are the most stable should be performed. To round out the analysis, a qualitative analysis should be performed looking at such factors as customer satisfaction and ease of implementation. Once a conclusion has been reached, a time-phased implementation schedule should be drawn up listing the major steps involved in transferring the distribution network from the existing system to the future system.

The seventh step in the distribution network planning process is selling the results to top management. This must be expressed so that management can understand the impact of the strategy on the total business. Not only should this communication express the finances relating to transportation and warehouse costs, but overall sales and customer satisfaction as well.

WAREHOUSE STRATEGIC MASTER PLAN

The second step in the DSMP is a warehouse strategic master plan. Warehousing is a dynamic, continuously evolving environment, in which the current plans and operations are constantly being scrutinized and molded to meet current and anticipated requirements. A successful warehouse maximizes the use of its resources while satisfying customer requirements; therefore its place in the DSMP is critical, since customer satisfaction is dependent on how the warehouse is designed, laid out, and utilized.

A warehouse's resources are systems/equipment, space, and personnel. Systems/equipment refers to information technology, dock equipment, material handling equipment, and unit load equipment. These comprise a large capital investment and must be selected and used so that the end result is an acceptable Return on Investment (ROI). Space costs include the cost of investment or lease and operating expenses, which includes taxes, insurance, maintenance, and energy. Personnel are the third resource. Approximately 50 percent of the costs of a typical warehouse are labor-related. Reducing the amount of labor and pursuing higher labor productivity will significantly reduce warehouse operating costs.

A warehouse strategic master plan is a set of documents describing actions to be accomplished and when they must be accomplished to satisfy the warehousing requirements of an enterprise over a given planning horizon. A closer examination of this definition reveals the important attributes of a good warehouse strategic master plan.

First of all, a good warehouse strategic master plan is a formal set of documents. It should not consist simply of ideas, thoughts, possibilities, desires, etc., that are casually recorded "somewhere," if at all. A good plan is a formal set of documents that have been created, collected, edited, etc., specifically as a strategic master plan of action. Common components of this set of documents include an implementation plan, a descriptive narrative, scaled facility drawings, and supporting economic cost and justification data.

Second, a good warehouse strategic master plan is action-oriented. Where possible, the plan should set forth very specific actions to be taken to meet requirements, rather than simply stating the alternative actions available to meet those requirements. Typically, scaled facility drawings should accompany each recommended action to illustrate what the facility will look like after a given action has been implemented.

Finally, a good warehouse strategic master plan should encompass a specified planning horizon. It should have a definite beginning and ending point. Typically, the planning horizon is stated in terms of years.

The general methodology for developing a warehouse strategic master plan consists of the following seven steps:

1. Document the existing warehouse operation.
2. Determine and document the warehouse storage and throughput requirements over the specified planning horizon.
3. Identify and document deficiencies in the existing warehouse operation.
4. Identify and document alternative warehouse plans.
5. Evaluate the alternative warehouse plans.
6. Select and specify the recommended plan.
7. Update the warehouse master plan.

The first step involves obtaining or developing scaled drawings of the existing ware-house facilities and verifying their accuracy. The accuracy of existing drawings should never be assumed. It should always be physically verified on the warehouse floor. Existing warehouse equipment should be identified and documented. The labor complement of each area of the warehouse should be determined and the general responsibilities of each person documented. Existing standard operating procedures should be scrutinized and compared against what actually takes place on the shop floor. This first step of the master planning process establishes a baseline against which recommendations for improvement can be compared.

Step 2 involves defining materials to be stored in the warehouse and the volume anticipated during the planning horizon. Items to be stored in the warehouse should be classified into categories according to their material handling and storage characteristics. Forecasts or production schedules should then be used to predict the storage volumes and turnover rates of each category of material over the specified planning horizon. Ideally, these volumes would be stated in terms of the unit loads in which the materials would be stored and handled.

The third step involves identifying potential areas of improvement in the existing warehouse operation. The potential for improvement may exist because the operation lacks sufficient capacity to handle future requirements or because existing facilities, methods, equipment, and/or labor forces are not the most efficient or effective available.

Step 4 deals with identifying alternative facility, equipment, procedural, and/or personnel plans that will eliminate or minimize the deficiencies identified in the existing warehouse operation. From these alternative plans-of-action will come the specific time-phased plan-of-action to be recommended for meeting the warehouse requirements over the given planning horizon.

The fifth step of the master planning process involves performing both an economic and qualitative assessment of the alternative plans of action. The economic evaluation should consist of a time-value-of-money assessment of the total life cycle costs of competing alternative plans- of-action. The qualitative assessment of alternatives requires that the alternatives be subjectively compared on such attributes as personnel safety, flexibility, ease of implementation, maintainability, potential product damage, etc.

Step 6 involves selecting the best of the alternative plans-of-action implicated by the economic and qualitative evaluations and specifying the recommended warehouse strategic master plan. The master plan will document the space, equipment, personnel, and standard operating procedure requirements of the warehouse over the planning horizon. In addition, scaled facility drawings should be included showing the recommended warehouse layout for all revisions recommended by the plan-of-action.

The first six steps of this procedure will result in a warehouse strategic master plan.

The strategic master planning process, however, will not be complete. To be successful, a warehouse must pursue continuous improvement by maximizing effective use of space, equipment, and labor, along with maximizing the accessibility and protection of the product. The warehouse requirements must apply not only to the finished goods function, but also to the manufacturing raw material and WIP functions. This may be accomplished through restructuring the functions of manufacturing warehousing.

TRANSPORTATION STRATEGIC MASTER PLAN

The third step in the DSMP is the transportation strategic master plan. The process is as follows:

1. Document transportation network requirements.
2. Identify delivery requirements.
3. Establish database.
4. Develop alternative transportation systems.
5. Model annual transportation costs.
6. Evaluate alternatives—define the ROI of each alternative compared to the baseline.
7. Select the best design for meeting the transportation requirements.

To accomplish the first step, gather information from all supply chain partners on the following requirements: freight classes and discounts, transportation operating procedures, and replenishment weight/cube. The delivery requirements (Step 2) should be time order placement to the receipt of the shipment. If the requirements are not identifiable, conduct a customer satisfaction gap analysis like that described in the strategic distribution network plan section. The database in Step 3 should include ship-to locations, weight of shipments, products ordered, and quantity ordered. Once this information is collected, supply chain partners can validate it.

Step 4 requires an organization to consider all transportation alternatives, including consolidating vendor shipments, centralizing slow moving items in one place, and establishing direct shipment by vendors. Today, carriers are providing more services and trying to break into new markets (e.g. intermodal services, containerization, import/export). When considering transportation, organizations must leverage their buying and negotiating clout to get the best rates and service possible.

Steps 5, 6, and 7 may be accomplished by following the procedures described in the section on the warehouse strategic master plan, but keeping in mind that they must emphasize transportation. Like the other two strategic planning processes, a transportation strategic master plan is never complete. It must be constantly updated and changed to meet the changes in the marketplace and the challenges of distribution today.

IMPLEMENTING THE DSMP

The DSMP is based upon a set of premises concerning future sales volumes, inventory levels, transportation cost, and warehouse cost. Requirements should be defined, analyzed, and evaluated and should result in the development of a specific set of strategic requirements.

Implementation is the process of translating an approved DSMP into a working system. It is the critical link in the project life cycle between planning and operation. Implementation is important because it is implementation that gives a good DSMP value. It is particularly important to an organization because it uses its scarce resources in order to realize expected benefits; a successful implementation makes a firm more competitive.

Implementation is like a train. It starts slowly with no seeming sense of urgency but quickly picks up steam. If not properly managed, it can get out of control. In other words, implementation requires a high degree of respect for today's distribution challenges. These are discussed in the following sections.

CHALLENGES IN DISTRIBUTION

It was once believed that to improve customer satisfaction, it was necessary to maintain high levels of finished goods inventory to prevent stock-outs. Although customer satisfaction levels may have been met, the actual competitiveness of an organization probably deteriorated because of higher inventory levels, resulting in increased carrying costs and decreased cash flows. Arbitrarily reducing inventories, as many organizations have attempted, can be equally damaging by reducing customer satisfaction levels. The challenge we all face is determining the right inventory levels that balance customer satisfaction with inventory investment.

Another challenge is the combination of marketing and its impact on SKU proliferation, and manufacturing and its desire to maintain long production runs. This combination can easily hinder all attempts to improve the distribution function. The final challenge lies in meeting management's desire to have the lowest cost distribution network with maximum customer satisfaction and high inventory turns.

Individually, these three desires are advantageous. A combination, however, will prove that they actually defeat one another. For example, maximum customer satisfaction for an organization might require a network of 10 DCs fed by three supply sources. This network will invariably require greater inventory levels and greater costs to operate than a network of three DCs. The real goals in distribution are to establish a level of customer satisfaction that meets or exceeds the customer's expectations and to minimize inventories and reduce costs. Once the customer satisfaction levels have been set, an organization must then rethink its distribution strategy and consider third party logistics, the push system vs. the pull system, and improved transportation management.

THIRD PARTY LOGISTICS

As companies and members of supply chains streamline themselves and concentrate on their core competencies, the popularity of third-party logistics (3PL) has increased. 3PL can be defined simply as using others to provide all or a portion of the logistics function. 3PL can offer flexibility, relieve frustration in managing non-core competencies, save money, and reduce inventory. However, 3PL can also reduce flexibility, contribute to frustration in core competency areas, cost money, and increase inventory. In other words, all outsourcing is not created equal.

There are three basic categories for 3PL provider competencies: asset-based, management-based (also called non-asset based), and integrated operators.

- Asset-based 3PL providers offer a dedicated logistics service through use of their current or expanded assets, including trucking operations, private fleets, warehouses, and so forth.
- Management-based providers focus on the management and technological services associated with providing logistics services. In most cases, these providers utilize the assets and the manpower of other organizations to provide logistics services and do not own transportation or warehousing assets.
- Integrated providers typically are outgrowths of a contract or for-hire logistics service supplementing their services with other vendors' service offerings.

While evaluating 3PL in your DSMP, it is vital to collect information, document it in a request for proposal, evaluate each candidate thoroughly, and use quantifiable criteria for choosing the appropriate 3PL provider. If 3PL is a good choice, the 3PL provider should be treated as a partner, with emphasis on communication, performance incentives, and a mutually agreeable contract.

PUSH VS. PULL SYSTEMS

Push systems are the byproducts of mass production. In a push system, sales predictions are used to determine the quantity of products to be produced and where they should be shipped. Forecasts are developed for sales regions, and products are manufactured and sent to the regions based on these forecasts. The emphasis is on using information about customers, suppliers, and production to manage material flow. In other words, the system pushes material through production according to schedules. Material is pushed from the production facility through distribution until the product reaches the customer.

Push systems depend heavily on the accuracy of forecasts. The advantages of a push system include

- Smaller manufacturing plant warehouses because the only warehousing activity performed at the manufacturing facility is staging
- Enhanced customer satisfaction as products are pushed to locations close to the customer
- Shipments from the plant to DCs in full truckloads (TL), which creates lower transportation costs.

The biggest disadvantage of a push system is the fact that it is based on regional forecasts, which are often inaccurate and many times unreliable. Inaccurate or unreliable forecasts can create

- Increased safety stock and, therefore, higher carrying costs
- Larger DCs to accommodate increased safety stock
- High stock transfer costs due to increased material handling, shipping, product loss, and damaged material
- Reduced product rotation
- Reduced crossdocking capabilities.

In a pull environment, an order from a customer generates an order from the DC, which then leads to a production run to replenish the plant warehouse. Therefore, in a pull distribution system, an inaccurate sales forecast has a less significant impact on the distribution system for two reasons. First, the forecast is not required within a regional area, only at the global level. Actual customer demands at the DC level trigger replenishment activity from the plant. Second, all fluctuations in demand are corrected by changing the production schedule at the production source, not at the regional DCs.

A pull distribution may experience significant potential problems including the following:

- Large on-site plant warehouses
- Slow order fill time (lower customer satisfaction level)
- Increase in less-than-truckload (LTL) shipments.

The larger onsite plant warehouses occur as a result of inventory being stored at the point of origin rather than at the point of distribution, as in a push system. These onsite plant warehouses increase the size of the plant, the plant warehouse staff, and may also enhance the plant's ability to expand production areas in the future. One way to reduce the size of the onsite warehouse is to shorten the production runs. In general, the investment in production equipment to increase capacity, improve efficiency, reduce maintenance, and reduce changeover time is better than investing in warehouse space.

A slower order fill time reduces the customer satisfaction level. As orders take longer to reach the customer, the future sales growth may slow or even decrease. Balancing the lead time for customer orders, inventory to fill those orders, and manufacturing lot sizes becomes extremely critical to limit the potential for lost sales.

The final potential penalty occurs when customer orders are placed. The combined demand for orders in a region generally does not equal full truckload (FTL) quantities. To increase the number of FTLs, additional orders need to be batched, which will further reduce response times. When orders cannot be combined to create FTL quantities to a DC, the transportation cost of an order increases significantly. Eliminating stock transfers between DCs as occurs in a push system may offset this additional cost. Now that sales forecast inaccuracies have less impact on a pull system, the following benefits can be realized:

- No stock transfers between DCs
- Lower safety stock
- Lower overall system inventory
- Direct plant to customer shipment opportunities.

The buffer inventory maintained at the plants serves as the system inventory and handles the reallocation of products to the DCs when sales fluctuations occur. This eliminates any DC to DC stock transfers. In addition, by storing all the inventory at the plants, the safety stock is reduced, because only systemwide sales fluctuations, rather than regional and systemwide sales fluctuations, affect product inventory. This in turn reduces the overall system inventory and the required warehouse space. The final benefit of a pull system comes from the opportunity for shipments to be made directly from the plant to the customer. For large customer orders from one plant, that plant can ship the order directly to the customer. This reduces costs of transportation and handling, reduces DC traffic, and improves response time and customer satisfaction.

A pull distribution system functions most effectively in an environment with a variety of production and distribution points and a large number of SKUs in the system.

HYBRID PUSH/PULL SYSTEM

In theory, SCS is a pull system. In reality, a hybrid, or synthesized, push/pull system is best for SCS to level manufacturing loads and address seasonality and peaks. A synthesized distribution system utilizes the push system for more popular SKUs and the pull system for the slower-moving SKUs. Consequently, slower-moving SKUs are stored at the production facility, and the more popular SKUs are transported in truckload quantities to DCs where they are distributed to customers.

The hybrid system has the following benefits over a push system:

- Reduction of stock transfers
- Reduction of safety stock
- Opportunities for direct customer shipments
- Improved opportunities for crossdocking
- Utilization of full truckloads
- Improved customer satisfaction.

An overall design strategy, therefore, requires both strategic and tactical refinements until the pull percentage is optimized.

TRANSPORTATION MANAGEMENT

Today, carriers negotiate any level of discounting they want, unlike in the days where the Interstate Commerce Commission established rates for them. Carriers are also free to act as

- Common carriers
- Contract carriers
- Brokers
- Freight forwarders.

They may act as several or all of these simultaneously, and suddenly, all the players on the field are wearing each other's uniforms. In other words, a common carrier may also be a freight forwarder. This is the same as Dan Marino acting as quarterback one moment and right tackle the next. This can create a type of distribution martial law.

Organizations try to increase control over their distribution expenses by reducing the number of carriers they use. This appears to be a smart idea, until the carrier goes on strike. Think of the UPS strike in 1997. It was unimaginable that UPS, of all carriers, would have employees that strike. Therefore, few distribution professionals had a contingency plan.

As a result, for 15 days in 1997, many businesses were crippled because there were no deliveries, slow deliveries, and wrong deliveries. During that time, UPS handled only 10 percent of its average 12 million packages per day, and competitors were unable to handle much of the other 90 percent. After the fact, the carrier estimated it lost five percent of its business, either outright or because they were downgraded and no longer other companies' carrier of choice.

To meet the challenges of Transportation Management, consider these guidelines:

- Specify free on-board, inbound freight. Ask suppliers for "freight collect" product costs in addition to prepaid freight charges by the supplier. This will enable the buyer to analyze logistics costs for items (otherwise, the freight cost is cleverly buried or bundled in the product cost, never to be uncovered) and provide additional flexibility in negotiating price and service issues.
- Renegotiate rates and services if they're more than one

year old. Many transportation providers are offering additional services and better rates to beat their competition. There is nothing to lose by testing and evaluating the waters every year.

- Assess the current transportation philosophy of the organization. The "if it ain't broke, don't fix it" mentality just does not apply here. Have you considered containerization for freight transport, for example? Imagine the amount of product that can fill a 20-foot-equivalent unit. For that matter, imagine never having to use overnight/priority shipping because distribution has properly planned and made the right freight decisions. What you did yesterday or even this morning might not provide competitive advantage this evening.

- Shop till you drop. A carrier decision takes into account more than just rates. Other considerations are service, a solid track and safety record, and geographic coverage and evaluation of the provider's financial status. Use carriers as resources and springboards for ideas. Make sure you compare.

- Regard purchasing and sales as allies. By forging strategic alliances within the four walls of the organization, transportation can be part of the solution rather than part of the panic.

- Evaluate the third party logistics concept (3PL) for non-core competencies. If warehousing and transportation functions are viewed as cost centers, 3PL might be the road to take.

- Remember that you are in business for your customer. One company I visited measured shipping errors as a function of customer complaint calls. A good day equaled a day with no calls. Unfortunately, the company didn't realize that no calls might have meant that the customer simply gave up on them and sought out another supplier altogether. Being proactive with customers (e.g., creating surveys, calling them for feedback before they call you) rather than reactive serves to unite customer and company more completely.

- In addition, management should periodically review those metrics that have been chosen to monitor their business to determine if those metrics are still representative of their current business practices or if they should be changed.

3PL OUTSOURCING CRITERIA

Quantifiable criteria that may be used to evaluate 3PL candidates include

- Customer satisfaction—check references and perform site visits to both the provider candidate and its customers. Will the third party provider seek and use input from your customers to improve the level of satisfaction? Will the provider be able to maintain and exceed current levels of satisfaction?

- Warehouse management systems—does the provider use information technology to operate its business effectively? Can it develop, install, and operate a better system than the one you are currently using? How will your system and theirs be integrated?

- Flexibility—can, and will, the provider change with your needs and your customer's needs?

- Buildings/Facilities—consider the availability, location, and utilization of dock capacity, lighting, personnel services, fire protection, and outside service aaes.

- Financial Depth—does the candidate have excellent credit and bank references? Is the financial statement solid?

- Geographic location—how does the candidate's geographic location make it strategically advantageous?

- Personnel depth—is there sufficient expertise and quantity to keep your company well serviced?

- Continuous improvement philosophy—is continuous improvement embraced and practiced at every level of the operation?
- Cost—how does the cost of service compare with other candidates of equal capability?

WHY DISTRIBUTION SYNTHESIS IS A CORE COMPETENCY OF SCS

The characteristics of distribution synthesis are
- Understanding the importance of customer requirements and satisfaction when designing a distribution network
- A DSMP that defines the requirements for an efficient and effective distribution system
- Proper utilization of 3PL
- Economic and qualitative evaluation of all viable alternatives based on specific, weighted criteria before any distribution network decisions are made
- Use of a hybrid push/pull system of distribution to maximize customer satisfaction and optimize manufacturing efficiency.

These characteristics generally indicate distribution synthesis for one organization. However, if a company has the knowledge to implement them internally, then that company has the knowledge to implement these characteristics for the entire supply chain. All distribution decisions (e.g., number and location of DCs, inventory levels, optimal order cycles and fulfillment rates, and order procedures) are then based on an SCS, rather than SCM or a traditional logistics environment. That is why distribution synthesis is a core competency of SCS.

13

SCS AND PARTNERSHIPS

"It is probably not love that makes the world go around, but rather those mutually supportive alliances through which partners recognize their dependence on each other for the achievement of shared and private goals."

—Fred Allen

Imagine the morning of Catherine, a typical commuter in Washington, D.C. She drives her Isuzu Trooper, the result of an alliance between Ford and Isuzu, to a gas station. There she pumps gas that is the product of an alliance between Shell and Texaco and pays with it on a credit card co-branded by Royal/Dutch Shell Group and Mastercard. Once she arrives at her office, she drinks a cup of Starbucks coffee she purchased at the Barnes and Noble around the corner from her building. Later, she will book a flight through Star Alliance, a global alliance between United Airlines and seven other carriers.

Partnerships are everywhere. The Internet, regulatory approval, deverticalization, global competition, and the need to replace risks are driving an alliance explosion, particularly in business-to-business (B2B) e-commerce. For example, in the first quarter of 2000, Ford, GM, the Nissan-Renault alliance, and Daimler-Chrysler announced a venture where they are linking to put their procurement needs on a single electronic trade exchange, creating the world's largest e-marketplace. This announcement followed the November 1999 announcement that Ford and GM were creating separate electronic trade exchange systems, which did not yield the desired reuslts. Now, the two companies Ford and GM had chosen to put their supply chains on the World Wide Web will collaborate to create this new e-trade system. Sears, Oracle, and French retailer Carrefour SA are creating a similar venture for the retail industry.

Some of these partnerships will fail and others will succeed. The ones that fail will be those who create a communications system with all the IT bells and whistles but only use it to foster traditional supplier/customer (manufacturer/wholesaler/retailer) relationships. I said the same thing about ECR in my book *Genesis*. The ones that succeed will be the ones that adopt SCS and use the B2B IT capabilities to assure quality communications.

DEVERTICALIZATION—CREATING THE NEED FOR PARTNERSHIPS

A jack of all trades and master of none—that is why a vertical organization does not contribute to SCS as well as it should. Vertical organizations own more of their supply chains and therefore focus less on core competencies. This was an acceptable proposition in SCM, when link optimization was tantamount to supply chain success. For example, vertical food conglomerates own farms, processing plants, manufacturing facilities, and warehouses. Acquisitions were seen as an effective way of growing market share and profitability.

What do these conglomerates do best when they're highly verticalized? Consumed by doing everything in their niche, they forget what was really at the heart of their strategic plan. The result? Mediocrity in many areas, and excellence in none.

Companies "deverticalize" by selling and outsourcing major supply chain segments while retaining control of their core business. Deverticalization can eliminate weak links in the supply chain and allow core divisions to grow, but it should never be done without a time-phased strategic action plan. An action plan enables companies to see the big picture of where they are headed and what functional strengths will take them to higher market share and competitive advantage.

What happens when deverticalization occurs exclusive of an action plan? Organizations tend to choose price but want high quality and wind up disappointed. Developing a master plan will certainly rein in the wheeler-dealers and enable the company to move in the direction of their strategic vision without a lot of bumps in the road.

Not using a hand does not mean cutting it off, an analogy that holds true for companies that deverticalize. If a non-core competency is outsourced, organizations must audit performance of the third party regularly for continuous improvement. Supply chain partners must be held to a specific standard (e.g., supplier certification programs such as those enacted by AIAG, the Automotive Industry Action Group). No one has to lose control of the function just because someone down or upstream is doing it.

Peak-to-Peak Performance begins with defining core competencies. Highly verticalized conglomerates cannot label everything a "core competency" and expect to succeed in this changing business climate. SCS begins with the notion that there are others in the supply chain who can perform functions better than you and inversely, who rely on you as well. This is why partnerships are so critical in SCS.

In Chapter 10, I explained the three customer tiers and identified the highest tier of customers as partners. In actuality, they are more than preferred customers; they are supply chain partners. In other words, you want to create partnerships with them, because they are an essential ingredient in operational success and continuous improvement.

Achieving the true partnerships needed for SCS is somewhat like the dating that leads to marriage. There's a meeting, then a date, then more dates. There is the time when both partners decide that they only want to date each other. If all goes well, there is an engagement and a wedding date is set. If the engagement is a success, then the wedding takes place. This all takes time and it has to be done right. Suppose you go to a bar tonight and someone who hasn't met you before asks, "Hey, want to get married?" Most likely you would either think that person wasn't serious or that person was crazy. If you decide to accept the proposal, then both of you are crazy.

Marriage does not end this process. Marriages continuously change and develop. I've been married for more than 31 years. The relationship my wife and I have is different now than it was thirty years ago. It has continued to evolve as we have evolved from a young couple to parents of two adults and a 15-year-old. And it doesn't stop here. It will keep changing as long as we are both alive.

It also takes time to create the relationships that lead to true partnerships. They are not created over night and require a great deal of intimacy. The business equivalent of a couple dating is the move to a partnership with a "customer-driven" organization. The next step is invincible customer satisfaction, which is the business equivalent of "going steady." To move beyond this relationship, the partners must step up their commitments to one another. Then the partners must begin significant planning for the partnership, just as if they were planning a wedding. The ultimate commitment is a true partnership.

This chapter defines true partnerships, discusses the challenges of true partnerships, the prerequisites to true partnerships, describes how to create a true partnership, and demonstrates why partnering is a core competency of SCS.

TRUE PARTNERSHIPS

To understand true partnerships, you must keep these things in mind:

1. When similar companies in the same kind of business band together to pool their resources to conduct research, evaluate technology, or lobby for a political position, they have not created a partnership. Instead they have created a consortium.

2. When companies lose their independence to become one corporate entity, it is not a partnership. It is an acquisition or merger.

3. When companies work together to pursue a specific, single-focused business objective, this is not a partnership. It is a strategic alliance.

4. When two companies form a separate entity with joint ownership to pursue a specific business objective, they have a joint venture, not a partnership.

5. A long-term relationship based upon trust and a mutual desire to work together for the benefit of the other partner and the partnership is a true partnership.

As you can see, it takes two committed organizations to have a true partnership. Each true partnership requires a supplier and a customer who are both ready for partnership. True partners invest in the long-term partner relationship that is based on trust and a mutual desire to work together for the benefit of the other partner and the partnership; there are No Boundaries separating their abilities to share information and requirements. Both organizations in the partnership are independent, but each retains its own identity to assure maximum innovation and creativity.

WHY ALLIANCES CAN MAKE MORE SENSE THAN ACQUISITIONS

- Flexibility and informality promote efficiencies
- Access to new markets and technologies
- Ability to create and disband projects with minimum paperwork
- Multiple parties can share risks and expenses
- Partners can retail their independent brand identification
- Working with partners possessing multiple skills can create major synergies
- Rivals can often work harmoniously together
- Alliances can take different forms, from simple R&D deals to huge projects
- Ventures can accommodate dozens of participants
- Antitrust laws can shelter cooperative R&D activities.

—*Business Week,* October 25, 1999

The characteristics of a true partnership are

- The partners reject the "arm's length" mindset, i.e., that business relationships should be based on antagonism, leveraging, hammering, and negotiating.
- The partners are committed to long-term relationships based on trust and a true understanding of their partner's business.
- The partners believe in sharing of information, planning, scheduling, risk, rewards, problems, solutions, and opportunities.
- The partners believe in working together toward improvements in quality, lead times, new product development time, inventory accuracy and management, and cost control.
- The partners believe in building on each other's strengths, increasing their partner's business, and investing in the long-term partnership relationship. Due to this commitment, the partners will deal with fewer and fewer suppliers.

- The partners believe in systems integration and the independence of their organizations while still retaining their individual identities to assure innovation and creativity.
- The partners believe in frequent communications at all levels of the organization and that partnership proximity is important and will be mutually addressed.
- The partners believe in getting their partners involved early in any new innovations and working with their partners with the utmost flexibility to assure the best overall performance of the partnership.

In other words, true partnerships are long-term collaborative relationships based on trust and a mutual desire to work together for the benefit of the other partner and the partnership.

THE CHALLENGES OF TRUE PARTNERSHIPS

Because a partnership is a true investment of time, money, and reputation, there is a lot at stake. Forming a true partnership requires discarding the traditional relationships common between organizations today. These relationships are characterized by an "arm's-length" mindset. Limited communication flows vertically within the two companies and only between the companies through the sales staff and buyers. Even then the focus of this communication is usually on problems, not their causes, correction, or continuous improvement. These factors contribute to extended lead times, higher costs, and a relationship that ignores the supplier's creativity.

Therefore, the key challenges to forming true partnerships exist in the areas of trust, communication, and organizational and cultural change.

These challenges can be overcome. A recent alliance between Ford and UPS demonstrate how two partners overcame a compensation challenge. Ford and UPS Logistics Group, a subsidiary of UPS, are developing a system to reduce the time it takes for vehicles to move from the assembly line to the dealership by 50 percent. They are revamping Ford's network of road and rail carriers and adding an information system that will make it easy to track individual vehicles through a Web site. The challenge the partners faced was compensation—who would be paid for what tasks—and they came up with an innovative solution. Between 100 and 150 UPS employees and 30 and 50 Ford employees will manage the system together, and UPS will be compensated based on how it helps Ford meet speed and efficiency goals. As more true partnerships are embraced in this millennium, such methods of overcoming challenges will become the norm.

TRUST

Trust is the key ingredient in a partnership. Trust between partners takes time and happens as a result of many positive interactions. From trust, relationships grow, trust progresses to respect, and respect fosters the willingness to listen. From this listening comes understanding, concern, participation, and then open communications. Since open communications lead to positive reinforcement for even greater trust, without trust there is no partnership.

It is important to note that trust does not occur between companies, but between people. Therefore, partnerships are not really about companies, but about people, and those people must be committed to making a partnering relationship work, whether it is a marriage or a partnership between a supplier and a customer. When employees are viewed as people who are part of the whole process, when previously proprietary information is shared, and when everyone shares the benefits of success, then employees develop trust in the organization and the cycle of success continues. When this kind of trust is developed within an organization (organizational change), the employees are better prepared to apply the same kind of trust to their formally antagonistic relationship with customers/suppliers (cultural change).

COMMUNICATION

The success of partnering efforts depends on the effectiveness of communication. Today's technology enables an instantaneous, continuous flow of information within and between organizations, which is discussed in Chapter 14. Care must be taken not to place too much emphasis on this technology while ignoring human interaction. It is important to have frequent and planned face-to-face interactions within the company and between partners. There must, therefore, be specific points of contact between the companies and assurance that they are committed to keeping the lines of communication open and anticipate potential problems.

ORGANIZATIONAL AND CULTURAL CHANGE

The biggest challenge in creating true partnerships is overcoming the existing paradigms of partnerships. These existing paradigms are the byproducts of organizational culture, which may be compared to a personality. For example, several years ago, we began working with clients on establishing partnerships. A major grocery chain retained us and selected three firms who did private labeling for them, and expressed the desire of forming partnerships with them. The first firm produced juice, and their leadership was progressive but cautious. The second firm produced jellies, syrups, and sauces, and their leadership was secretive and resistant. The third firm produced cookies, and their leadership was open and eager to participate.

Well, the results were predictably very mixed. The cookie firm established a very meaningful partnership that netted huge benefits to both our client and the cookie manufacturer. The juice firm also established a meaningful partnership with the grocery chain and this partnership netted huge benefits for our client and the juice producer. However, the partnership took twice as long to be established and took twice as long to net results.

Unfortunately, the jelly firm did not establish a partnership. In fact, the lack of trust between the firms resulted in the deterioration of their relationship, the decline of activity, and the reduction in profits to each. The issue that is so amazing about these three relationships is the grocery chain and our process were consistent in all three relationships. The culture of the three firms, however, dictated different responses to our partnership initiative, and thus a wide diversity of results. Culture is a key component of establishing partnerships and must be understood and developed to achieve those results from partnerships that should be achieved.

To overcome a traditional culture that takes the existing view of partnerships, there must be organizational and cultural change (i.e., the Revolution discussed in Chapter 8). This may be accomplished with a Business Process Continuous Improvement (BPCI) philosophy. BPCI is a leadership-driven process of collaboration that uses teams and a shared Model of Success to change company culture and operating style. Organizational teams are created across job functions, product classes, and organizations that consolidate, integrate, and share organizational responsibilities. Once BPCI is used within one organization to achieve cultural change, then companies may use it to develop a joint Model of Success for forming a true partnership.

PREREQUISITES TO PARTNERSHIPS

CEO commitment and leadership are core ingredients for a true partnership. Only the CEO has the power to commit the resources to form partnerships and to break down the barriers to resistance. The CEO must foster a climate that allows the organization to define its relationships with its suppliers and customers in new and creative ways. The CEO and upper management must make decisions that support the philosophy of continuous improvement, and they must communicate this philosophy throughout their company as well as outside it. Any choice made based on price alone sends a clear message that while the company may say they want cultural change and partnerships, in reality, it is "business as usual." Too often leadership gives its commitment only to be distracted by more short-term issues. When leadership focuses elsewhere, the partnership initiative frequently founders. The wavering of top leadership's attention is one of the most frequent causes of failure of partnering initiatives.

Another cause of partnering initiative failures is the tendency of leadership to proceed before the organization is ready. Frequently, once the initiative is identified, leadership often wants to charge forward and make improvements immediately. They tend to want to launch an intense effort before everyone understands the initiative, much less before they become aligned with it. Leadership expects committed employees and committed suppliers to follow.

A better approach is to develop a strong consensus and necessary supporting structure at the top before beginning the improvement effort. Senior leadership needs to spend time off site working through the issues. This allows all concerns to be discussed until there is near total acceptance of the initiative, scope of actions, necessary cultural changes, rewards and recognition, supporting systems, and the process of implementing the mission statement.

Another prerequisite for a true partnership is developing a succeed/succeed mindset for the partners. What has historically held partnerships back has been a succeed/fail (or win/lose) mindset. Those that have this mindset believe that if the other party succeeds, then they fail, and so they do not cooperate. They view their partners as opponents, not collaborators. In a succeed/succeed partnering mindset, the supplier is totally focused on helping its customer achieve success because the supplier believes that is the only way to succeed. Powerful relationships develop because suppliers and customers are focused on making each other successful.

The final prerequisite for true partnerships is for each organization to develop an internal team-based structure and then take it outside the organization. In fact, the partnering process can be thought of as the application of team-based development between organizations. Organizations with such a structure respond quicker to change and thus are truly able to collaborate to deliver quality and customer satisfaction at a lower cost. Team-based organizations make true partners because they are better equipped to respond to strategic opportunities.

CREATING TRUE PARTNERSHIPS

A true partnership is the successful application of the collaboration process between organizations. The objective of creating true partnerships is to create the same synergy between organizations that was created from the collaboration process within an organization.

Striving to create long-term partnerships means first understanding that the term "relationship" is not synonymous with partnership. Growing a relationship into a partnership, and ultimately into an SCS partnership, means realizing that

- No two relationships develop the same way.
- Relationships evolve as comfortable bonds between individuals.
- A positive chemistry must exist between two parties to create a relationship.
- Partnerships evolve from understanding hopes, dreams, and an anticipation of a bright future.
- Each party must know themselves and understand what they are seeking from the partnerships.
- Acceptance by indirectly involved parties (e.g., stockholders, government) is as important to the perpetuation of the partnership as acceptance by directly affected parties.
- The relationship, at its core, has interest in the well-being of the other party as well as the well-being of the partnership.
- Expectations of how the relationship will develop must be articulated.
- Compatibility is key to a long-term relationship.

Identifying potential true partners should be based on the opportunity for additional contribution to profit over a five-year planning horizon. This applies to both a customer looking at its suppliers and a supplier looking at its customers. The focus should be on building trust, then communicating clearly, and finally, creating the Peak-to-Peak Performance discussed in Chapter 8. As these relationships continue, the escalation of trust, openness, and success will naturally lead to the sharing of Models of Success and strategic business plans.

Also part of the partnership process is chartering a Partnership Initiative Team. The purpose of this cross-functional team to establish an official collaborative relationship, determine the objectives of the partnership, and develop a mutual plan for the partnership. As a result, the identity of suppliers/customers will become blurred until they have No Boundaries—first individuals, then teams, then entire companies will be true partners. Without boundaries, the partners will act as a whole to improve, grow, and prosper, while still maintaining their own corporate identities.

WHY PARTNERING IS A CORE COMPETENCY OF SCS

You cannot have SCS without true partnerships. As discussed above, true partnerships are based on the principle that sharing information openly, communicating requirements extensively, and involving alliances early in processes will provide competitive advantage and strength to an organization. SCS takes the concept of a true partnership and extends it beyond the organization to the supply chain. This increases the challenges discussed earlier, because managing relationships throughout an extra- or extended enterprise adds to the complexity.

With SCS, the intimacy of a true partnership is among four or five partners, who comprise the supply chain to be synthesized. These four or five intimate partners are committed to the SCS process, have win/win mindsets, and have team-based structures in place. They have determined specific criteria for evaluating the partnerships as well as potential new partners. They also know, as SCS partners, that they have a long-term relationship that must provide mutual benefit through open communication, continuous improvement, and a focus on the customer. Therefore, they communicate with one another on causes of problems, corrections, and continuous improvement, rather than on the problems themselves. SCS partners also believe that the challenges they face in partnerships—trust, communications, and culture—must be overcome to secure competitive advantage; improved performance of the TOTAL supply chain is necessary through partnerships; the keys to partnership success are integration, information, and interaction; and it is important to benchmark partnership activity for continuous improvement.

THE VALUE OF PARTNERSHIPS—PALLET MANAGEMENT SYSTEMS

Pallet Management Systems specializes in asset recovery of non-standard pallets, servicing the building materials, fibers, chemical and plastics, and high-value electronic markets. Pallet Management Systems has 15 locations and 450 employees and the key to the company's success is simply to take a relationship-oriented approach to each client account, focusing on long-term solutions for their customers rather than quick fixes.

Pallet Management Systems understands that outsourcing on the part of their clients requires recognition of non-core competencies, and the approach their partnerships in the same way. By partnering with 3PLs, plastic packaging manufacturers, and RFID/barcoding technology integrators, the organization can provide an entire solution to an asset recovery issue.

For example, through partnerships with RFID vendors, Pallet Management Systems can help clients enable the supply chain more effectively, by providing more upstream information real-time. Once the packaging or pallet reaches a certain value, it justifies closer tracking as it travels from one manufacturer to the road to the customer and back again. Product and packaging are linked through bar coding or electronic tags, and such information as how quickly it moves allows companies to plan asset recovery strategies based on proven trends, rather than on hypotheses.

The key to the success of SCS partnering is to assure alignment around shared goals. Building on the assumption that intra-organizational alignment has been achieved, the next step is to ensure that this spirit of cooperation and collaboration is extended throughout the supply chain. In other words, there must be a supply chain culture that creates and nurtures Peak-to-Peak Performance through teaming, true partnerships, and the proper use of IT and the Internet. That is why partnering is a core competency of SCS. Organizations are more willing and better prepared to partner with the supply chain if they have already learned how to partner with another organization.

14

SCS AND COMMUNICATIONS

"Today we have access to technology that greatly facilitates the exchange of...information. We can share methodologies with supplier-partners in ways that just weren't possible five or ten years, ago, which results in dramatically faster time-to-market."

—Michael Dell

In 1998, the J.L. Kellogg Graduate School of Management at Northwestern University and a team of professors from MIT conducted a communications survey and concluded that companies would save millions each year if only they would communicate more efficiently with supply chain partners in matters of inventory control and forecasting. When you think about that conclusion, you can see that it is a "no-brainer." When you set out to integrate business processes and disparate entities in the supply chain, you must communicate. It is vital to the success of all SCS core competencies. And if you communicate effectively and continually across the supply chain, with No Boundaries, then you will achieve SCS, and not only will your company and its partners save millions of dollars, but they will see improved customer satisfaction.

Today, organizations have a variety of options for communicating openly from direct links to virtual private networks (VPNs), which transport data over secure Internet channels as if they were private lines. They also have a wide range of information systems available to them for strategic, tactical, and technical purposes. These include

- Accounting
- APSs
- Budgeting
- Enterprise resource planning (ERP)
- Finance
- Fleet maintenance
- Forecasting
- Freight rate management
- Inventory management and control
- MESs
- Order entry, processing, and management
- Procurement
- Production planning and control
- Salesforce automation
- TMSs
- WMSs.

If I had written this book in the early 1990s, I probably would have covered all these systems, outlined the underlying technology that helped run them, suggested means by which they could be integrated with a comment on the expense of this integration, and moved onto the next chapter. And in a few years, I would have had to issue a reprint. Why? Because it would have been obsolete.

Information technology (IT) has fundamentally altered business and production processes in the last decade. Communication systems and communications options are changing radically today, thanks to the Internet (and its most popular user interface, the World Wide Web), which is being used to create new partnerships and alliances almost daily because it connects all means of communication together inexpensively. This is virtually eliminating the expense factor that figured so highly in former attempts at integration.

THE DIFFERENCE BETWEEN THE INTERNET AND THE WORLD WIDE WEB

The terms Internet and World Wide Web are often used interchangeably, due to a common misconception that they mean the same thing. In actuality, they do not.

The Internet is a global network that connects millions of computers. In 1999, the Internet had more than 200 million users worldwide, and that number is growing rapidly. More than 100 countries are linked into exchanges of data, news, and opinions. Each Internet computer, called a host, is independent. Its operators can choose which Internet services to use and which local services to make available to the global Internet community.

The World Wide Web is a system of Internet servers that support specially formatted documents. The documents are formatted in a language called HTML (HyperText Markup Language) that supports links to other documents, as well as graphics, audio, and video files. In other words, users can jump from one document to another simply by clicking on the links. Not all Internet servers are part of the World Wide Web. Because of this, the World Wide Web should be viewed as a subset of the Internet. As such, it is an ever growing part of the Internet, but it will never be the same entity as the Internet.

Actually, there has been so much excitement lately over the fact that major manufacturers, software companies, and retailers are using the Internet to create B2B alliances and electronic trading communities that an important point is being lost. You can link as many suppliers, retailers, and customers as you want through the Internet, but if you don't use SCS communications, your partnerships and alliances will fail. So, the main thing to remember about SCS and communications is that the specific information systems to perform the links are not important. What is critical is that the Internet be used to foster SCS partnerships as described in Chapter 13 so that everyone along the supply chain can use SCS communications to achieve success.

This chapter will focus on the changes brought about by current IT developments and the explosion of the Internet rather than defining simple communications. Therefore, after discussing SCS communications, it introduces and relates the following to SCS: extending electronic data interchange (EDI); business applications; extranets; and Collaborative Planning, Forecasting, and Replenishment (CPFR).

SCS COMMUNICATION

SCS communication is simultaneous, instantaneous, and multi-directional to allow all supply chain partners to work at the same time rather than sequentially. This eliminates inventory buffers and accelerates the flow of cash. It also allows dynamic planning, which replaces the outdated practices of long-term forecasting. It makes strategic information available to all partners so that all have contact with the customer and are aware of changing needs and trends. They can then respond in unison to these needs and trends.

SCS communications must be clear, relevant, open, and honest. Also, all parties must be linked, and the information requirements of each must be integrated into the communication process; that is why the Internet plays a key role in SCS communications. There must be clear, concise, and ongoing communications at the outset as well as a willingness to share key information, withholding nothing, regardless of how close the relationship is. At the same time, there must be complete acceptance of the equality and interdependence of the players. Each has a leading role in one or more functional areas, no matter how they are interconnected. These basic communication principles are then maintained throughout all supply chain processes.

Important to the success of SCS communications is the elimination of information silos. Information must be shared throughout the supply chain's communications network. If information is not shared and accessible to all links of the supply chain, then SCS cannot be achieved. SCS communications therefore require systems that can manage and transmit all types of data and information along the supply chain to make sure all partners are receiving accurate, timely, and high-quality information. It is critical that these systems exploit the power of the Internet, for that is what allows SCS communications.

Although Internet-linked information and communication systems are the most critical requirements for SCS communications, to be completely effective, SCS communications systems must also facilitate face-to-face and interpersonal communications to maintain the trust necessary for true information sharing and collaboration. This means intelligent participation in and management of person-to-person communications consistent with supply chain partner needs.

Building an SCS communications system requires integrating three essential types of capabilities. The system must be able to handle day-to-day communications and transactions and e-commerce along the supply chain, which can help align supply and demand because orders and daily schedules are shared. The system must also facilitate planning and decision making, supporting demand and shipment planning necessary for distributing resources effectively. And finally, the system must provide tools like an integrated network model that will allow strategic analysis. Electronic connectivity via the Internet provides the backbone for this communications system, which will greatly reduce transaction costs as orders, invoices, and payments are handled electronically and lower inventories through vendor-managed inventory programs. The key is ensuring the continuous flow of information.

THE VALUE OF COMMUNICATIONS—HYUNDAI MOTOR AMERICA

Hyundai Motor America was in a quandary. Only 20 percent of Hyundai owners were returning to dealerships for replacement parts after the warranty expired, and Hyundai wanted to help its dealerships and also make ordering parts easier and more cost-effective for its car owners.

The organization decided to reach its supply chain members through an extranet/Web site. Customers, body shops/garages, and dealerships can search for 30,000 individual parts numbers with diagrams. A shop manual for installation will be added soon to facilitate matters. For example, hot links will be created to connect a specific part to its installation instructions. For car owners, parts can be shipped to a residence/business or to a nearby, participating Hyundai dealership. Repair shops can use the Internet to sign up with dealerships to set up wholesale accounts. Dealerships can use e-mail to confirm customer order status.

Traffic on the site has been heavy, and Hyundai expects that two-thirds to three-fourths of its dealerships will ultimately sign on to the service. George Kurth, the national manager of parts supply, distribution, and systems planning at Hyundai, notes: "If we can get information to customers with older vehicles, we will make them happy, and that is very important."

FIVE SUPPORTING TECHNOLOGIES OF SCS COMMUNICATIONS

Five supporting technologies that specifically add value, accuracy, and expediency to the SCS communications are

- Direct Link—telephoning and faxing are the most prevalent examples of direct link. No one is predicting the end of voice communication quite yet, but more accurate, faster, and cheaper methods of information sharing, involving less employee time and no paper shuffling, are outpacing direct link.

- Local Area Networks (LANs)—capable of transmitting data faster than telephony but over shorter distances, LANs connect users to expensive peripheral devices such as printers, allowing them to share these utilities. LANs also enable users to send emails and engage in chat sessions. The number of users on a LAN is limited; however, many LANs connected to one another can form a WAN.

- Wide Area Networks (WANs)—a system of LANs connected via telephone lines and radio waves makes up a WAN, which can span a large geographic location. Computers typically connect to a WAN through telephone systems, leased lines, or satellites. The largest WAN in the world is the Internet.

- Virtual Private Networks (VPNs)—a network accessible only to users with authorization. VPNs guarantee security through encryption (translation of data into a secret code) and other security mechanisms. An example of a VPN is typing a confidential password in that allows you access to your account on large sites such as Amazon.com. VPNs are usually connected to the Internet but operate separately from it. To be a part of this network, companies must pass comprehensive and rigorous security tests.

- Electronic Data Interchange (EDI)—what used to be a competitive advantage enjoyed only by large companies that could afford it, EDI is becoming more accessible, courtesy of the Internet. A protocol for the electronic exchange of business documents in standardized format between businesses, EDI is used globally by major corporations for communications with their trading partners. EDI has 300 transaction sets, three of which are purchase orders, invoices, and order acknowledgments. With its approved set of standards, called X12, EDI facilitates sharing of data between partners for buying, selling, and trading information.

THE VALUE OF USING THE WEB FOR SCS COMMUNICATIONS— LIZ CLAIBORNE

In November 1999, Liz Claiborne received *Consumer Goods Technology* magazine's award for leadership in technology at the Consumer Goods Information Technology Conference for the company's success in using technology to transform the corporation. By interweaving business strategy development with IT strategy, business process re-engineering, cost reduction, and pioneering in new technology, the firm developed numerous competitive advantages, including saving in operating costs, inventory, cycle time, and customer service.

One example of Liz Claiborne's technology leadership involves Web-enabling retail buyer. Liz not only build a front end that lets retailers order goods over the Web, but created a virtual showroom in which retail buyer can examine the goods remotely. It can even zoom in to inspect the stitching in a single button. The system will automatically develop customized assortment plans in both units and dollars over the Web, bringing the expert services of Liz account teams to small, specialty retailers. Another example is Liz Claiborne's global supply chain management and new product development. The company is not just taking some inventory out with improved management of supplier and sourcing, but is now creating a global real-time network of 250 Web-linked suppliers in 38 countries.

—*Consumer Goods Technology,*
February 2000.

The Web's destiny is to become the great communications equalizer among organizations. No longer will small companies with small company budgets be forced to accept inaccurate communications, slow communications, or no communications. Companies do not even need T-1 lines (a popular leased line option for businesses connecting to the Internet) or streaming video to be on top of their supply chain communications. They simply need a browser and an Internet Service Provider (ISP) who understands their needs. The Web is certainly leveling the playing field when communications is the issue, and it may signal the lessening of significance the five supporting technologies will have on future SCS communications.

EXTENDING EDI

Currently, EDI is one of the most popular forms of extraorganizational communication and is viewed as effective enough to ensure a small role in Internet and e-business initiatives, but not without support from and synergy with e-business technologies.

Some of the e-business technologies that can be used to enhance EDI are

- XML—an easy-to-write, cross-platform software language that enables designers to create their own customized tags to provide functionality not available with HTML. XML is expected to extend the ability for users with workstations to become part of the trading community through its Web-based form applications.
- Internet-based business communication/Web-form EDI— enables smaller businesses to communicate with larger trading partners through web site access. A user goes to a web site, pulls up the appropriate form, and enters data. Some systems verify the data against a database.
- Extranets and intranets—private and semi-private web sites for companies and their commerce partners. These are discussed later in this chapter.
- Business-centric portals—portals that centralize an industry (e.g., PlumbingonLine for the heating, ventilation, and air conditioning industry). Many business-centric

portals are procurement-related.

- FTP (file transfer protocol)—a protocol that is gaining in popularity with small companies for point-to-point EDI delivery. There are companies that provide specific connections for firms that wish to send EDI data from a translator to a designated server, completely bypassing a VAN mailbox

- E-mail—used to send unstructured material.

- Application to application—also known as buy-side e-commerce for business-to-business (B2B) applications. This is discussed in the next section.

- Application service providers (ASPs)—a new type of Internet service. ASPs lease server space to companies so that they may host software applications without buying a server (which is a high-dollar item). In some cases, ASPs will lease applications to companies. Software and hardware maintenance are the ASP's responsibility.

EDI will eventually be replaced as a communications method, but this will take several years. One common scenario is using EDI for business partner communications and the Web for consumer-based communication. This scenario, however, is not an example of SCS communications. SCS communications are seamless, whereby all communications occur over the Internet and on the Web, and not in various forms for various functions.

BUSINESS APPLICATIONS

In the last few years, applications vendors and developers have begun using the Internet and the Web to create enhanced relationships between supply chain partners. They have concluded that user interfaces for systems will be browser-based and that client/server applications will be replaced with thin clients, multi-tier applications, XML, and enterprise-strength Java. To these ends, they are developing applications that exploit the separation of business data and databases from the user, manage various forms of messaging, and break up data into small chunks for better security. These applications are called business applications. They allow one company's systems to communicate directly with another company's systems through the Internet or over the Web.

Business applications are also being developed to meet the needs created by a shift from client/server computing to multi-tier computing. Multi-tier computing, also referred to as three-tier computing, is computing on at least three tiers: client, application server, and back-end legacy systems. Business applications reside on the middle tier (the application server) and are used to connect and integrate data from back-end, legacy systems and present them in a format that can be accessed by any client. The client can be anything from a workstation to a palm-sized computer.

Examples of business applications include those used to design extranets, supply chain planning and execution systems, spread-sheet macro languages, packaged simulation tools, enterprise information systems that support key business processes and house enterprise data, and data warehousing systems. These applications rely on the "write once, use everywhere" principle of the Java language. They are non-proprietary, which means they may be used by different operating systems (e.g., Unix, Windows, Solaris) and clients across enterprises.

The most common use of business applications is to connect ERP systems to the supply chain. ERP has been very useful to organizations, but it does little to remove the boundaries between supply chain partners. Because many corporations have invested significant amounts of money in their ERP systems, they are reluctant to dispense with them altogether. Business applications not only allow communication between ERP and peripheral applications; they can also integrate them. Proponents of Collabo-rative Planning, Forecasting, and Replenishment would argue that this is a waste of time, but to companies who have been satisfied with ERP, integration represents middle ground between "business as usual" and huge investments in new communica-tions systems.

SCS communications most often are between existing systems rather than new systems. Business applications and their Web-based interfaces and languages allow communications between all kinds of systems. And because the Web is becoming the great equalizer for information and communications, the use of business applications to promote SCS communications will not only continue to increase, but also continue to reinvent themselves. Therefore, business applications are critical components of SCS communications.

EXTRANETS

The use of extranets for B2B communications continues to grow. An extranet is an intranet that is partially accessible to authorized outsiders, and it may be accessed through an address on a Web browser. The difference is that an intranet resides behind a firewall and is accessible only to people who are members of the same company or organization, whereas an extranet provides various levels of accessibility to outsiders. A valid username and password accesses the extranet and that identity determines which parts of the extranet may be viewed.

Extranets resulted from the revolution in business communication created by the Web. Companies used to design and use one system or systems for communicating inside the business and another system or systems for use *outside* the business. The Web changed that whole communications paradigm. With the Web, companies can develop applications that work across multiple communications platforms, using the same methods to communicate internally, externally, and all across the supply chain. Extranets are one of those methods.

In 1996, then CEO of Netscape Jim Barksdale stated that there was a rush to exploit extranets for extraorganizational communications and cited his own company as a pioneer in this trend. The trend has not been quite the rush he claimed, but it is enjoying healthy growth. A major boost in their use occurred in late 1999, when Ford and GM announced that they were creating extranets that would allow their supply chain partners to communicate with them and share information. This announcement indicates that extranets are seen as vital for success in today's marketplace.

Extranets have the following characteristics:

- Information is stored across the expanse of the communication network rather than in separate data repositories.
- Those sending and receiving information are as close as

they can be to one another, with neither electronic nor human filters.

■ Individuals can act on information as soon as it is available.

These are similar to the characteristics of SCS communications. Those wishing to achieve SCS and use SCS communications, therefore, should embrace extranets. They should include them in their communications strategies, because they reduce expenses and cycle times—two key requirements for SCS.

COLLABORATIVE PLANNING, FORECASTING, AND REPLENISHMENT

The Voluntary Interindustry Commerce Standards (VICS) Association developed Collaborative Planning, Forecasting, and Replenishment (CPFR) to meet what many companies and communicators felt was a deficiency in ERP systems, which integrate some functions but do not address the entire supply chain. CPFR allows collaborative processes across the supply chain, using a set of processes and technologies that are:

■ Open, yet allow secure communications
■ Flexible across the industry
■ Extensible to all supply chain processes
■ Support a broad set of requirements (new data types, interoperability with different database management systems, etc.)

This is a radical departure from traditional planning, forecasting, and replenishment. Usually, computer software is used to compare historical trends and generate a forecast. Anyone with additional information revises the statistical forecast in hopes of improving accuracy. CPFR, however, allows customers to contribute to the generation of numbers and participate in other parts of the process. It changes relationships from buyer/seller to partner/partner as customer and purchase orders become collaborative forecasts and replenishment orders.

The key requirements for CPFR are real-time, global, secure, and simultaneous communication. Real-time information is a requirement because if the information is outdated, it has no value and creates both a delay as partners wait for reorder point replenishment and a buildup of inventory. Global communication is necessary, because CPFR is a worldwide phenomenon. Secure communication is critical for establishing trust between multiple supply chain partners. Simultaneous communication is a requirement because the information must be shared between all interested parties at the same time; otherwise, the supply chain remains time-phased and linear, rather than nimble and responsive.

As the Internet (and World Wide Web) has grown from a place to advertise to a place to do business, so has the idea that it can provide the means for meeting CPFR communication requirements. For example, the technologies used in the first CPFR prototype were all Internet technologies:

- SIL—a data definition and data manipulation language that allows for dynamic message translation.
- SMTP (simple mail transfer protocol) and S/MIME (secure/multipurpose internet mail extensions)—communication and security protocols. SMTP is a protocol for sending e-mail messages between servers. S/MIME is a secure version of MIME (a specification for formatting messages so that they can be sent over the Internet) that supports the encryption of e-mail messages so that they are secure.
- Standard HTML, Java, and JavaScript—Web and application development languages.

Also, Logility, a supplier of collaborative value chain solutions, has announced I-Community, a Web-based collaborative network of trading partners that uses the Internet to collaborate on sales forecasts and replenishment plans. The Internet technology it uses is XML, which structures and defines data for easy integration between systems and eliminates the need for value-added networks (VANs) or translation hardware.

In some ways, CPFR is like SCS. It has the succeed/succeed mindset required for SCS partnerships, and, in fact, it could even be defined as an SCS partnership. Its communication requirements are the same as those for SCS, for SCS demands realtime, simultaneous, global, and secure communications. Also, CPFR realigns the notion of competitiveness from company vs. company to supply chain vs. supply chain. From all these standpoints, CPFR can be seen as a microcosmic SCS. It therefore would make sense to think of using CPFR as a tool to achieve SCS.

THE VALUE OF CPFR—HEINEKEN, USA

Heineken USA is using Web-based CPFR solution to exchange demand forecasts and other beer distributors, freeing it from setting up EDI links. The solution was prompted by the fact that Heineken faced a 12-week lead-time in product delivery in 1998. To meet customer demand better, Heineken re-engineered its business processes and implemented an Internet based collaborative planning system called HOPS (Heineken Operational Planning System), developed by Logility, Inc.

HOPS was designed to improve communication between Heineken and customers, correct irregular inventory management, and improve business systems and processes. This Web-based solution links all 450 Heineken distributors to Heineken USA so that they can share forecasts, order products, improve communication, and replenish beer supplies through the Internet using Web browsers and ordinary desktop PCs. No special hardware or proprietary network connections were required.

Using information technology to coordinate and manage all aspects of the supply chain, from order processing to shipping, to fulfillment and delivery, Heineken USA reduced lead time from 12 to 4 weeks (67 percent within six months and has seen a 20 percent increase in sales force productivity. Using HOPS, Heineken can calculate demand and manage the supply of product to meet it, with an improved forecast accuracy of 12 percent (from 20 percent to 8 percent error). The national importer can now guarantee on-time deliveries within five percent of confirmed orders.

CORE COMPETENCIES CONCLUSION

The last eight chapters have discussed the eight core competencies necessary for achieving SCS—Change, Peak-to-Peak Performance, Total Operations, Customer Satisfaction, Manufacturing Synthesis, Distribution Synthesis, Partnerships, and Communications. Once these competencies are mastered, you have the tools and skill sets necessary for achieving SCS. The next and final part of this book addresses how to use them to achieve SCS.

15

SCS Supply Chain Design, Planning, and Execution

"Before beginning, plan carefully."

—Cicero

A ny number of organizations interested in satisfying the ultimate customer may comprise a supply chain. These include organizations that farm, mine, or render raw materials; those that refine the raw material into usable materials; and those that process the materials into products or product components. Also part of the chain is the final manufacturing organization that brings all the components together in a consumer-ready product and the organizations at the other end of the chain—the packaging and distribution channels that lead to a consumer and the retail operation that presents and sells the merchandise. The scope of a particular supply chain can involve more than 25 links, each with a specific interest and influence on the supply chain.

The question that arises when all this is taken into account is, "Is it possible for organizations to develop an initiative that addresses such a wide range of requirements?" The answer is, "Yes." The initiative is SCS, and it is indeed possible to achieve. Achieving SCS incorporates supply chain design, supply chain planning, and supply chain execution (Figure 15.1).

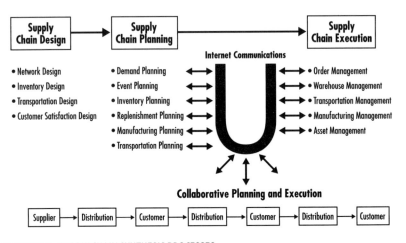

FIGURE 15.1: SUPPLY CHAIN SYNTHESIS PROCESSES

Supply chain design means designing for SCS. It is the first step in the process and is design at the highest level. It is comprised of network design, inventory design, transportation design, and customer satisfaction design. Supply chain planning follows supply chain design. It is a detailed planning process that is created to meet the needs identified in the supply chain design process. Supply chain planning involves demand planning, event planning, inventory planning, replenishment planning, manufacturing planning, and transportation planning. Supply chain execution is the final part of the process of achieving SCS. Supply chain execution involves the systems that address SCS in real time: order management, warehouse management, transportation management, manufacturing management. The Internet plays a role in the process as well—it is the means by which communications between supply chain planning and supply chain execution are accomplished.

This chapter addresses the components that comprise supply chain design, supply chain planning, and supply chain execution.

SUPPLY CHAIN DESIGN

Supply chain design means organizing network, inventory, manufacturing, warehouse, and transportation activities to meet the satisfaction requirements of the ultimate customer. Supply chain design, therefore, answers the following questions, which you may recognize:

1. How many facilities do we need?
2. Where should the facilities be located?
3. How much inventory should we stock?
4. What customers should be satisfied by what location?
5. How should the customers order from us?
6. How should we order from vendors?
7. How frequently should shipments be made to each customer?
8. What transportation methods should be utilized?

These questions are the foundation for the DSMP necessary for achieving distribution synthesis.

NETWORK DESIGN

In the past, locating distribution centers closer to customers was perceived as the way to provide superior customer satisfaction. Today, population shifts, labor costs, local business climates, and the global economy all contribute to the relocation and realignment of logistics networks. For example, supply chain partners may need to design multi-level logistics networks. One company met the demands of two large companies with long lead times and small regional firms that needed products delivered within 24 hours. The company created three full-stocking DCs and then set up multiple crossdocks located near the small companies for fast-moving products.

Network design involves innovative thinking because a logistics network is a complex entity comprised of several partnerships, some of which may be third party (e.g., 3PL). Where shared customers and similar geographic approaches result in redundant networks, combining logistics for both complementary and competing third-party companies is one way to provide a lower-cost, supply chain-wide solution. Network design for SCS, therefore, should follow the steps presented in Chapter 12 as part of the DSMP. The SCS network must also be flexible to meet various customer satisfaction requirements. This flexibility requires more robust design methods enabled by real-time decision-support tools that can support distribution and manufacturing synthesis.

For example, one of our clients wanted to consolidate 14 U.S. distribution centers down to three existing centers. The client asked us to reconfigure the three selected centers and to add the required material handling equipment systems and procedures while meeting an aggressive six-month implementation schedule. (The timeline is an example of the speed required for SCS projects these days.) We recommended that our client install a pick-to-light system and a WMS, relocate and upgrade the existing pickline, add a conveyor, and add to and densify storage.

The result of implementing our recommendation was a 400 percent improvement in throughput capacity, a 50 percent increase in storage capacity, and improved material flow and improved inventory accuracy. This is an example of how, as supply chain partners reduce DCs and coordinate these reductions, less inventory and less total storage space are required. Reducing the number of DCs will also reduce total operating costs and will facilitate automated technology implementation. Supply chain partners may even share DCs to reduce the numbers along the supply chain, providing partners with substantial logistics savings.

INVENTORY DESIGN

Inventory design answers the third question of supply chain design: how much inventory should we stock? SCS inventory design should be done with an eye to inventory reduction, inventory accuracy across the supply chain, and the effective combination of push and pull systems. The inventory design requires the answers to the following questions:

    1. What inventory turns and levels are desired?

2. What fill rates are desired?
3. What safety stock levels are desired?
4. What products will be seasonal?
5. How will we keep slow-moving inventory to a minimum and, eventually, eliminate it?

Inventory accuracy is critical to successful inventory design. When a company's inventory is not 100 percent accurate, then its supply chain partners, especially buyers and planners, often protect their positions by carrying extra stock, which is never reduced later; the result is ballooning inventory. It's a vicious cycle. To improve inventory accuracy, supply chain partners must have a planned program for inventory accuracy in place.

A program for inventory accuracy should include automatic identification systems (AutoID), vision systems, weight checking, and cycle counting. AutoID eliminates the chances of data entry errors because they are based on the automatic recognition of bar codes or characters. Vision and weighing systems perform counts on materials being processed in and out of DCs, and the counts may be used to reconcile with recorded activity to identify errors. Cycle counting classifies items into categories of dollar value turnover and establishes a cyclical inventory schedule. Specific items in each category to be counted in a given week are randomly chosen, counted, and the actual count reported. Cycle counting also maintains statistics on the percentage of good counts vs. total counts made to gauge the accuracy of the inventory records. Cycle counting can help trace and correct discrepancies because the comparison of actual inventory levels with inventory records occurs continually.

TRANSPORTATION DESIGN

Because multiple means of transportation are readily available, transportation design requires careful consideration. Supply chain partners must look beyond internal transportation needs to all supply chain transportation needs. They must identify any transportation problems at the outset, asking questions like, "How satisfied are we with the cost and service of our present means of transportation? Is additional transportation support necessary for our supply chain partners?" Actual transportation activities for the supply chain should be compared to the supply chain ideal for transportation and adjustments made.

The process to be used to design the transportation system for the supply chain is part of the DSMP outlined in Chapter 12. Briefly, the steps are:

1. Document transportation network requirements.
2. Identify delivery requirements.
3. Establish database.
4. Develop alternative transportation systems.
5. Model annual transportation costs.
6. Evaluate alternatives—define the ROI of each alternative compared to the baseline.
7. Select the best design for meeting the transportation requirements.

CUSTOMER SATISFACTION DESIGN

In Chapter 10, I listed three questions that must be answered to achieve customer satisfaction. To repeat, these questions are

1. Who is the customer?
2. What does the customer want?
3. How do we increase customer satisfaction?

Customer satisfaction design is based on the answer(s) to the third question, which include reduced costs, increased quality, promotion of teamwork, and responsiveness.

Designing for reduced costs requires the simplification of products and manufacturing and distribution processes, reduced scrap and rework, and the elimination of unnecessary operating procedures. It also means identifying information and other technology requirements that will improve process control and productivity. Designing for increased quality means determining the requirements for doing things right the first time, identifying the standards and process control for all levels, and identifying the requirements for focused training that will help employees in the entire supply chain produce quality products and services.

THE VALUE OF A WMS SELECTION PROCESS—MERCK & CO.

Selecting the right WMS is critical to achieving SCS. For example, in a search for a warehouse management system that would provide secure pharmaceutical lot control, Merck & Co. examined the products of 28 WMS vendors with specific criteria: cost, system design, operational design, implementation and scheduling capabilities, related experience, company strength, and support capabilities.

"When we searched for a WMS system, we knew it had to be able to handle these issues in a variety of different ways," said Walt Taylor, Project Manager for Merck. "For instance, the Distribution warehouse has many floor locations and we cannot afford to put different lots in the same location. Therefore, it was extremely important to us that our lots be kept separate."

After reviewing each of the WMS products based on the established requirements, Merck was able to select the correct system—MARC—for its Supplies (Raw Materials) and Distribution (Finished Goods) warehouse facilities, which total more than 300,000 feet. The WMS provides each lot with corresponding quality control status. For example, a lot can be rejected, released, or quarantined. The lot control functionality allows Merck to track this specific information and determine where a particular lot should be stored. As a result, Merck's inventory accuracy level has increased to more than 95 percent, the inventory turnover in the Distribution warehouse is greater (80 to 90 percent), warehouse space is better utilized, speed and efficiency have increased, and support of functional areas has improved.

Customer service design must promote teamwork throughout the supply chain. Partners must communicate their ideas for meeting customer satisfaction requirements and staying competitive. Customers must also be asked specifically to identify their requirements for satisfaction. Identifying customer satisfaction Requirements of Success must be a team effort. Set up cross-functional teams to ensure operational understanding and support.

Customer satisfaction cannot be achieved if supply chain partners are not responsive to the needs of the ultimate consumer. This means identifying the methods that will reduce cycle times and increase flexibility. Once these have been determined, supply chain partners should then identify the means by which they will handle changes in customer requirements.

Customer satisfaction design should also answer the fourth, fifth, and sixth supply chain design questions I presented at the beginning of this chapter:

- How should the customers order from us?
- How should we order from vendors?
- How frequently should shipments be made to each customer?

Other considerations include those in the DSMP as described in Chapter 12. They will aid in putting together a plan executable across the supply chain that is based on a clear, consistent vision for satisfying the ultimate customer.

SUPPLY CHAIN DESIGN PRINCIPLES

There is no single, best design for an integrated supply chain; however, there are principles that can provide guidance for supply chain partners designing such a system with No Boundaries. These partners should

- View the supply chain design activity as an integrated process and appoint an SCS leader who oversees it.
- Conduct regular sales and operations planning meetings that continuously review performance and operating concerns.
- Operate with a single forecast and replenishment plan, instead of separate plans for finance, sales, logistics, and manufacturing.

- Centralize process administration as well as the inventory and replenishment requirements planning, but leave responsibility for forecasting and weekly/daily line scheduling close to the source.
- Build flexibility into the system through SCS manufacturing, quick set-up and changeover capabilities, cellular manufacturing, "postponement" principles, and a rapid and efficient planning cycle time.
- Use decision-support tools, real-time information, and integrated software in the design process.

The most important thing to remember about supply chain design for SCS is that it is not only collaborative, but it is also a synthesized process. There must be No Boundaries between the elements of supply chain design because each element relies on the other for a complete, ultimate customer-centric design.

SUPPLY CHAIN PLANNING

Once a supply chain design is complete, the functions necessary for making it a reality must be defined and executed. Supply chain planning defines the operations plan to bring the supply chain design to life, and supply chain execution is comprised of the functions necessary for executing the plan. The Internet is the means by which they communicate.

Supply chain planning is the planning for the placement of the right materials at the right location at the right time. In many supply chain situations, the partners work together well on the design stage but become bogged down in the planning stage. This can be for several reasons, one of which is that they are focusing on software and not on synthesis. Secondly, they have not eliminated all boundaries. To achieve SCS, there must be No Boundaries. Supply chain partners must focus on results, using demand planning, event planning, inventory planning, replenishment planning, manufacturing planning, and transportation planning.

Demand planning is a method of forecasting based on past orders. Event planning is forecasting based on the future. Inventory planning identifies the optimal balance between inventory and desired levels of customer satisfaction based on industry best practices. Replenishment planning determines the proper timing to achieve the inventory plan. Manufacturing planning involves the scheduling of the manufacturing operation, and transportation planning puts in place the transportation procedures to bring the supply chain to life. These various components of supply chain planning must be linked and cumulative (e.g., demand planning and event planning should be used to drive inventory planning, which in turn should drive replenishment planning, etc.) for SCS to be achieved.

HOW BOUNDARYLESS IS YOUR ORGANIZATION?

The following table describes the behavior of organizations whose supply chain planning and execution have No Boundaries.

	No Vertical Boundaries	No Horizontal Boundaries
Speed	Most decisions are made instantly by those closest to the work and acted on in hours, not weeks	New products or services are getting to market at an increasingly fast pace
Flexibility	Managers at all levels routinely take on front-line responsibilities as well as broad strategic assignments	Resources quickly, frequently, and effortlessly shift between center of expertise and operating units
Integration	Key problems are tackled by multilevel teams whose members operate with little regard to formal rank in the organization	Routine work gets done through end-to-end process teams; other work is handled by object teams drawn from shared centers of experience
Innovation	New ideas are screened and decided on without fancy overheads and multiple rounds of approvals	Ad hoc teams representing various stakeholders spontaneously form to explore new ideas

	No External Boundaries	No Geographic Boundaries
Speed	Customer requests, complaints, and needs are anticipated and replied to promptly	Best practices are disseminated and leveraged quickly across country operations
Flexibility	Strategic resources and key managers are often "on loan" to customers and suppliers	Business leaders move regularly among operations in different countries
Integration	Supplier and customer representatives are key players in teams tackling strategic initiatives	There are standard product platforms, common practices, and shared centers of experience across countries
Innovation	Suppliers and customers are regular and prolific contributors of new product and process ideas	New product ideas are evaluated for viability beyond the country where they emerged

DEMAND PLANNING FOR SCS

Demand planning for SCS must use the Internet to link all customers, suppliers, and distributors in the supply chain so that they may collaborate in this planning process. For example, sales and marketing partners should be able to generate a business overview integrated with the numbers that actually drive the manufacturing, purchasing, or inventory plans. Or they should be able to use the Web together to create virtual views of the future that encompass each phase of each product's life cycle.

Demand planning for SCS must synthesize customer demand with inventory supply processes, such as an organization's manufacturing, distribution, or procurement activities. It should also reconcile demand history, existing customer orders, POS data, market forecasts, and other information. This creates a clear, comprehensive overview of demand by item, location, customer, and/or group that may be used to determine demand patterns and ensure an executable plan that is compatible with all manufacturing processes in the supply chain.

EVENT PLANNING FOR SCS

Supply chain partners must anticipate and accommodate business events. Event planning for SCS should monitor and control events that affect supply and demand—promotion, competitive strategies, profitability, and sales volumes. This substantially reduces the possibility of unforeseen events adversely impacting supply chain relationships and profitability.

Event planning for SCS requires network-based technologies to predict and be prepared for the effects of seasonality or promotions, which enables supply chain manufacturers to adjust production to match changing demand. Promotion analysis and management can determine what activities work best and what their effect on profitability and sales will be. They may also analyze ongoing profitability and identify cost components.

INVENTORY PLANNING FOR SCS

Inventory planning for SCS must feature advanced simulation capabilities, automated rules-driven analysis, and time-phased support. These elements help manufacturers and distributors reduce inventory costs while still meeting all customer requirements—even when they vary by product, group, or other criteria.

Inventory planning for SCS should allow supply chain partners to set key inventory targets and goals for the entire supply chain—targets and goals based on meeting the needs of inventory design. Inventory planning for SCS must also facilitate decisions related to safety stock/inventory minimums and maximums, inventory turns, replenishment frequency and order size, seasonal production, and manufacturing plans. Online ABC analysis to help focus inventory investment on key items that contribute most to customer satisfaction and increased profitability is also necessary. Service level targets, ordering rules, and policies then can be applied automatically to every item across the supply chain.

REPLENISHMENT PLANNING FOR SCS

Replenishment planning for SCS is basically an advanced continuous replenishment strategy that uses the Internet for collaboration as well as extensive EDI support for automatic ordering, replenishment, invoicing, and shipping. It must utilize Distribution Requirements Planning (DRP) so that supply chain organizations can maintain a complex distribution network while remaining connected with partners and customers. With DRP, supply chain organizations can view inventory from several perspectives, including actual demand data, future distribution needs, and replenishment commitments. The benefits include faster inventory turns, maximized inventory levels, and the ability to match profitability to customer response—all of which are requirements outlined in supply chain design.

Other features of replenishment planning for SCS should be automatic detailed item planning to balance loads and orders, advanced simulation that determines the effects of SKU policy changes, new supply chain behavior, and constrained DRP. Constrained DRP factors in customer orders, forecasts, and inventory policies for each item so that inventory may be distributed equally when customer demand exceeds availability. As a result, customer orders are always synchronized with the most current supply chain manufacturing schedules.

MANUFACTURING PLANNING FOR SCS

Manufacturing planning for SCS is based upon finite-capacity scheduling. This constraints-based planning, which was discussed in Chapter 11, helps achieve the inventory, customer satisfaction, and network requirements identified in the supply design process. It balances manufacturing processes and resources with demand priorities and supply chain objectives, which in turn simplifies and accelerates the creation of long-range strategic capacity plans, tactical master production schedules, and operational schedules on the plant level.

Manufacturing planning for SCS requires the accurate modeling of the production environment. This allows it to determine such supply chain capacity constraints as equipment capabilities, intermediate storage limitations, shop floor calendars, and raw material availability easily. It can also identify chain production constraints, which include integrating multi-step operations, product sequencing, changeovers, and inventory policies. Once these constraints are determined, SCS manufacturing planning uses scheduling algorithms to produce the best plans quickly. There must be a built-in warning capability that notifies the supply chain when capacities have been exceeded, resources are unavailable, and shortages in raw materials exist or other conflicts occur. This manufacturing planning helps supply chain partners and organizations identify bottlenecks, and sourcing problems before they occur, providing the responsiveness that is key to customer satisfaction design.

Supply chain partners and organizations should use manufacturing planning for SCS to make quick, informed decisions while balancing capacity, customer satisfaction, and profitability. This may be accomplished by the integration of activity-based costing with production schedules. Intelligent decisions can then be made about sourcing production in the most effective production lines or plants in the supply chain, as well as about the factors that directly affect the bottom line, such as reduced inventory levels and holding costs, or the trade-offs between line changeover and carrying costs.

TRANSPORTATION PLANNING FOR SCS

Transportation planning for SCS must generate shipping plans that balance network design, customer satisfaction design, and transportation design requirements. It should evaluate the carriers, costs, transit time, and options outlined in the transportation design identified in the supply chain design process. This is accomplished by consolidating rate and carrier databases for all transportation nodes and enterprise shipment requirements. From there, supply chain organizations can quickly create a load plan consisting of multi-stop truckloads, pooled shipments, round trips, and continuous moves. This plan allows supply chain organizations to select the best mode and carrier, while satisfying delivery dates and minimizing costs. They may also consider the pros and cons of private or dedicated fleet vs. contract or common carrier using business rules, order characteristics, carriers and rates, time windows, and transit time.

SCS transportation planning must feature improved carrier utilization, consolidated freight, maximized discounts, and automated planning to reduce transportation costs for inbound, outbound, and interfacility moves and to improve productivity. Most importantly, SCS transportation planning exploits the narrow delivery windows created by customer continuous replenishment programs to meet increased demands for smaller, more frequent shipments.

SUPPLY CHAIN EXECUTION

Supply chain execution represents the real-time physical movement and accounting of materials and products through the supply chain. As I stated earlier, the components of supply chain execution are order management, warehouse management, transportation management, manufacturing management, and asset management. Order management accepts orders and passes them to the appropriate systems for fulfillment. Warehouse management supports the activities of the facility by

- Interfacing with material handling equipment
- Reporting on performance in areas such as customer satisfaction, inventory and order accuracy, space utilization, labor productivity, and item activity
- Guiding the warehouse through the daily activities to maximize efficiency and effectiveness.

Transportation management focuses on controlling costs and managing inbound, outbound, and intra-supply chain goods movement. Manufacturing management assures the efficiency and effectiveness of the manufacturing operations. Asset management is the maintenance of assets so that supply chain execution can occur without downtime created by faulty equipment.

Like the components for supply chain planning, for these supply chain execution components to be effective in SCS, they must have specific characteristics. These are detailed in the sections below.

ORDER MANAGEMENT FOR SCS

Order management for SCS must validate and prioritize customer orders so that they may be processed quickly and distributed to the manufacturing, warehousing, and transportation systems. Order management for SCS is often linked to customer satisfaction departments; within its functionality it can develop expected shipment and delivery dates based on product availability. The information it generates serves as a benchmark against the requirements determined by demand, event, inventory, and replenishment planning and may be used to adjust those requirements over a period of time.

WAREHOUSE MANAGEMENT FOR SCS

Warehouse management for SCS should substantially increase the accuracy of shipping and inventory functions by maximizing information and material flow through the warehouse. Warehouse management systems (WMSs) must supply an improved view of warehouse operations, which results in reduced operating costs, better space utilization, and improved customer satisfaction. The WMS should be real time, AutoID-based, and use radio frequency (RF).

Warehouse management for SCS must be flexible, scaling information and features based on the size of supply chain warehouses, their levels of automation, and the capabilities of their workforce. Warehouse management for SCS should link supply chain planning with logistics functions—tracking goods as they are received, stored, and shipped. The WMS should include performance analysis tools that allow supply chain organizations to make decisions regarding customer satisfaction, inventory, and productivity that may affect supply chain planning. It also must support crossdocking, random storage, compliance labeling, and lot/expiration date control.

Warehouse management for SCS demands a WMS that can be used for integrating industry best practices with specific warehouse requirements. A distributed processing approach that supports a wide variety of facilities, including national and regional DCs is another requirement. This approach helps supply chain organizations meet the demands of continuous replenishment strategies defined during supply chain design and supply chain planning, while reducing inventory and transportation costs.

TRANSPORTATION MANAGEMENT FOR SCS

With more than 70 percent of a company's logistics costs related to transportation, an organization that implements transportation management for SCS will find its ability to track shipment inefficiencies, unnecessary costs, and excess labor benefits the supply chain's bottom line. Transportation management therefore must include load planning along with carrier selection, rating, and pick-up scheduling. Other capabilities are shipment consolidation, freight payment, and claims management.

It is critical that transportation management for SCS be tightly integrated with transportation planning to ensure that the best plans are efficiently scheduled, executed, and tracked. Automation that can handle load tendering, shipment documentation and confirmation, shipment status, and even freight auditing and payment is vital. It supports various methods of tendering shipments, including EDI, email, phone, and fax, and can update carrier responses immediately. Shipment information can be sent to a WMS or an OMS to initiate order fulfillment.

Also required for transportation management for SCS are freight auditing and payment control functions. Freight bill information can be entered either electronically or interactively and audited against shipment data to prevent duplicate payments, erroneous billing, and carrier overpayment. Through these functions, authorized payments can be sent to accounts payable systems and payment to carriers that do not issue a freight bill can be done through a self-invoicing feature. They can allocate freight costs at multiple levels, including cost center, customer, product group, or SKU. All information about orders, shipments, and payments are integrated into a shipment database, which offers order, shipment status, and carrier performance visibility, and allows comparisons between planned and actual shipment costs.

This database must be shared electronically so that all supply chain partners can accurately distribute shipment costs, measure profits, and improve supply chain performance.

MANUFACTURING MANAGEMENT FOR SCS

A critical aspect of SCS is tying manufacturing to all other functions in the supply chain and, specifically, to the requirements of manufacturing planning. Manufacturing management for SCS, therefore, must accept data forecasts, costs, and planning information from supply chain planning systems so that the information may be balanced with shop floor activities, allowing on-the-spot decisions.

Manufacturing management for SCS should feature online transaction processing. Materials, processes, and employee activities are tracked in real time and if adjustments to the manufacturing plan are necessary, they are identified and recorded. SCS manufacturing management also provides seamless integration of disparate enterprise data and system applications, as well as integration with suppliers, distributors, and customers.

Manufacturing management for SCS requires Advanced Planning and Scheduling (APS). APS delivers schedules that respect both resource and material constraints and provide bottleneck identification and throughput management. Because constraints no longer impact processes, the APS enables organizations to exploit the full functionality of their equipment. Backward, forward, and concurrent scheduling help maximize productivity.

ASSET MANAGEMENT FOR SCS

Asset management for SCS must enable partners within the supply chain to share information about asset-specific data, procedures, and methods. If one site encounters and solves a problem with a particular asset, other sites also benefit from having that solution at their fingertips. By providing asset history for statistical analysis, a consistent application of key performance indicators for identifying and implementing maintenance best practices is possible. The capability of consistent cross-functional training inherent in asset management for increases productivity and reduces costs.

The supply chain is about more than pushing raw materials in one end and pulling finished goods out the other. Indirect materials also play a part in the process. Without maintenance, repair, and operations purchases, nothing would move through the supply chain. Emphasis is rarely placed on the maintenance functional area, but its role in SCS is critical. Asset management software solutions provide tools to handle everything from requisition generation to invoice matching. Typically they do not communicate directly with prospective suppliers. They cannot check pricing and availability on a real-time basis nor can they execute a purchase order with the supplier. A purchasing agent or buyer must do the legwork: Checking catalogs, calling suppliers, and faxing purchase order forms. This is all changing. Auction websites are available for many products and services under the MRO umbrella, and other sites offer comparative bidding and analysis so companies do not have to indiscriminately and blindly hop from auction site to auction site looking for the best deal.

Organizations must realize that e-, the great leveler for competitive advantage, must be part of the asset management functionality. MRO must not be viewed as a cost center but rather as a tool for success.

SUPPLY CHAIN PLANNING AND EXECUTION PRINCIPLES

During supply chain planning and execution, businesses must look outward. External applications—e-commerce, customer relationship management, and supply chains with industry-specific applications—help build SCS. Supply chain planning and execution therefore require the application of the eight core competencies of SCS, as well as the following qualities

- A focus on the customer
- An acceptance of partnering
- An aggressive adaptation of technology, such as e-commerce
- A belief in the process of teaming
- A focus on synchronized performance measures

- An openness to creativity and innovation
- A belief in the importance of having No Boundaries between the links of the chain.

These principles are block-and-tackle basics of supply chain planning and execution for SCS. Both depend on one another to assure the success of the supply chain.

Since SCS is a continuous improvement process, so are supply chain planning and execution. In other words, the results of supply chain execution affect supply chain planning because real-world events can change even the best-laid plans. It is good to review the supply chain planning components regularly and adjust them if execution warrants it. Supply chain planning in turn determines supply chain execution, and if it is altered, then the execution methods may also be altered. Therefore, there should be No Boundaries between supply chain planning and execution.

16

THE GLOBAL IMPLICATIONS OF SCS

"In today's world, where businesses are global and people are refining things down to the last cent of efficiency, you can't be all things to all people."

—Steve Rogel, CEO and Chairman, Weyerhaueser Company

Consider the Battle of Hastings in 1066 as the first time in history where the global implications of SCS met head-on with the traditional thinking about boundaries. In this renowned historical battle, William, Duke of Normandy, invaded Great Britain, defeated the Saxons, who were led by Harold, King of England, and took over the British monarchy. The battle was hard fought by both sides and many lives were lost, including Harold's.

When the final sword was thrust and victory achieved, William of Normandy did more than win the British crown; he effectively changed the course of history, of language, and of British culture forever. British nobility spoke French, not English, until nearly the 15th century; many resided on French estates as well. When you use the word "amicable" to describe a relationship or order "roast beef" at a restaurant, thank the Battle of Hastings, for the incorporation of French words into the English language would never have occurred otherwise.

So, on that October day in the eleventh century, Great Britain moved closer to Europe than it had ever been. No channels of water would separate it completely again from the continent. Information was being shared, alliances were being forged, political systems re-envisioned, and commerce between the nations of Europe strengthened. In effect, William was adding links to his supply chain (or rather, *souple chaeine*, the French words from which "supply" and "chain" are derived) beyond the rigid geographic boundaries of France to derive more competitive advantage.

Of course, globalization is better achieved these days with "point and click" rather than "invade and massacre," but the results are often the same. Strong, international supply chains are meant to shake things up, to make life more difficult for competitors. That is why SCS demands a global perspective. Business no longer ends at the U.S. border for American corporations. Success depends heavily on reaching foreign markets, and reaching full economic potential means reaching out to other countries and pushing aside boundaries to receive their goods and services in return.

This chapter discusses the trade agreement and regulations that drive the global economy, explains how information systems and technology support the global economy, and then puts both in the context of SCS.

REACHING OUT

The late Ron Brown, former U.S. Secretary of Commerce, once said, "We know free trade means progress for all people, and that with open markets come open systems." For much of the mid-twentieth century, American protectionist policies have run counter to Brown's statement. For example, after the U.S. hesitated to penetrate the Latin American markets, Europeans took a substantial interest in the Caribbean, capitalizing on its consumer, labor, and resource pools. Fortunately, in the last two decades, trade agreements have been established that encourage open markets. These were discussed in Chapter 2.

At the same time that these trade agreements were being made, new plans and laws, as well as broad enhancements to existing laws, were made to encourage closeness in partnerships and alliances, the testing of new waters like virtual business, and reaching out to neighbors beyond geographic borders. One such plan is the Global Information Infrastructure (GII). The principles of the GII are that the private sector should spearhead expansion of the Internet and e-commerce within a simple, consistent legal environment and with few government restrictions. Much of this plan emphasizes security and establishing a global "Uniform Commercial Code":

- Parties should be free to order the contractual relationship on their own terms and not the government's.
- Rules should be modified only as necessary to support electronic technologies.
- The process of developing rules should involve both high-tech industries and businesses that have not yet moved online.
- Rules will not assume or mandate a particular technology.

An example of broad enhancements to existing laws are the changes that have been made to the Universal Commercial Code (UCC). The UCC was formulated under the assumption that all trading would be through a paper medium, and therefore parts of it fail to address an electronic environment. Companies considering either a traditional EDI/VAN package or a more innovative EDI/Internet connection were lost on some issues. So, in response to these needs, some basic changes were made to the entire UCC. "Record" replaced "writing," and "authentication" replaced "signature." It also introduces the "electronic agent," which is a computer program (and eventually, an avatar) used by a party to communicate electronically without review by an individual. Choosing an electronic agent binds an organization to the actions of the electronic agent.

OTHER KEY REGULATIONS AFFECTING GLOBAL COMMERCE

In addition to changes in the UCC, the following laws, policies, and regulations, will influence e-commerce and by association, global trade.

- National Conference of the Commissioners on Uniform State Laws (NCCUSL) Electronic Transaction Act—this act recognizes the electronic record and agreement as substitutes for paper, assures that signature requirements can be met through electronic means, and modifies existing rules of contract law as they apply to transmission and receipt of communications.
- Electronic Authentication Act of 1997—this act affords e-commerce the same respectability and significance as paper-based commerce, within certain parameters.
- Electronic Commerce Security Act—this act establishes a legal infrastructure to facilitate the implementation of secure electronic commerce and record-keeping for business and commerce.
- General Usage in International Digitally Ensures Commerce (GUIDEC)—GUIDEC governs the use of public key cryptography for digital signatures and the role of a trusted third party (a certifier) in establishing that the key holders are who they say they are.
- United Nations Commission on International Trade Law (UNCITRAL) model—this model establishes rules and norms that validate and recognize contracts formed through e-commerce and supports the admission of computer evidence in courts and arbitration proceedings.
- International Institute for the Unification of Private Law (UNIDROIT)—this comprehensive source on the principles of international contract law has begun researching provisions designed to eliminate barriers to e-commerce.

Another enhancement to the UCC is Article 2B. Article 2B releases those engaged in EDI from needing a Master Trading Partner Agreement and then defines terms and phrases unique to e-commerce. The article also covers many important issues related to information technology and paperless communication. Clarifying terms is especially important, since the previous UCC did not cover, much less protect, e-commerce partners.

SCS AND THE GLOBAL REGULATORY ENVIRONMENT

Reaching beyond the geographic boundaries that separate nations is critical for achieving SCS. Businesses in Europe welcome and (informally) utilize the supply chain's potential more readily than their American counterparts—and Americans could learn much about trade alliances from them. Europeans then could benefit from American philosophies on information technology. European firms generally perceive replacing IT systems as a huge, costly undertaking, a mentality that runs counter to the U.S. continuous improvement philosophy.

Developing nations like Mexico, Poland, and China embrace foreign investment. These countries, often known for their adaptable, flexible attitudes, offer attractive opportunities in exchange for assistance in improving infrastructure and national welfare. Partnerships and alliances are at the heart of SCS, and global partnerships that encourage cooperation and collaboration between organizations in different countries are most effective in achieving SCS. The Star Alliance mentioned in Chapter 13 is an example of the type of global partnership SCS promotes.

As discussed earlier, trade agreements and changes to laws and regulations have been made to encourage such global partnerships. Also, plans like the GII that encourage the use and recognition of electronic signatures and authentication, the acceptance of electronic communications, and the promotion of efficient and effective e-commerce dispute systems can contribute to achieving SCS because these are indeed methods of doing business without borders.

Another product of this global regulatory environment that affects SCS by providing open, timely information is the Trading Partner Agreement (TPA). A TPA is a formal contract that fills in the blanks left by existing contract laws, rules of evidence, and issues of liability. Key elements are a statement of intent, a clarification of liability, security, signatures, and a receipt. The TPA, therefore, is a solution for preventing disagreements and misunderstandings—and is an attractive deliverable to offer supply chain partners new to the principles of SCS. Each should be unique, because each supply chain is unique, and care taken to tailor the agreement to the needs of each supply chain partner.

INFORMATION SYSTEMS AND TECHNOLOGY

Without information systems and technology, borders and boundaries would still characterize the global economy. The Internet has created a migration from the vertical enterprise of Henry Ford's day to the virtual enterprise. In this virtual world, managing the integration between organizations and those who provide those organizations with competencies outside their core competencies (e.g., manufacturing, logistics, sales, or distribution) requires technologies that can visualize and personalize. In other words, these technologies need the ability to identify each unique partner so that various terms and agreements are accessible for transactions over secure lines. These technologies include encryption, authentication, password controls, and firewalls.

The Internet offers these technologies and more. It allows companies to reach into new, global markets and create new ways to serve those markets by introducing the following:

- Channel management—creating new channels or enhancing existing relationships with channels through better information, speed, and service.
- Enhanced collaboration—achieving performance improvement with trading partners through simplified communications.
- Market making—creating new products and services.
- Knowledge management—sharing knowledge and techniques across the enterprise and with key trading partners to develop new products and conquer new markets.

With these new processes comes a need to manage information, including managing content, knowledge, and innovation, as well as the need to manage partner relationships. These needs have created a new type of global thinking such as

- Thinking in terms of revenue per employee
- Thinking in terms of Days of Supply (DOS) inventory (i.e., viewing inventory in terms of days and even hours)
- Thinking in terms of no Days Sales Outstanding (DSO), where the money from the customer is in the bank before suppliers are paid
- Thinking in terms of negative asset intensity (i.e., no capital investments to create business initiatives)
- Thinking in terms of return on marketing investment: "I can measure response in markets of one"
- Thinking terms of agility (i.e., time to market, cycle times, and response times).

SCS AND THE INTERNET

The new global economic rules created by the Internet achieve SCS in various ways. Projects that seemed impossible before the Internet created global connectivity can now become a reality. For example, the Internet and information technologies can be used to

- Promote a focus on employees as assets rather than expenses, using their knowledge to gain efficiencies or expand markets as they use the Internet to serve on cross-boundary teams
- Master customer relationship management through technology investments that link companies to the ultimate consumer
- Meld business processes together
- Create a place for the customer in the information infrastructure
- Manage virtual structures and create new financial models for them
- Design new compensation plans for employees
- Create security for safe navigation across web-based business communities

- Leverage various media to create brand and process recognition.

The Internet removes the boundaries that made the above capabilities difficult to achieve in years past because it is a form of communication that recognized No Boundaries. Communications can be sent to any area in the world in real-time. That is what makes the above list of strategies possible.

GLOBAL STRATEGIES

Innovative thinking is necessary to convince partners to leave protectionism behind and embrace the concepts of the new world economic order so that they may achieve SCS. Already, innovative thinkers in the automotive and electronics industries are developing strategies that may be used to promote these concepts. Not all strategies are similar, but they agree on four principles for promoting global supply chain initiatives:

1. Create a global supply chain vision. This vision must motivate employees and trading partners to view the world as their supplier through techniques designed to minimize and eliminate resistance to change, cultural biases, and stereotypes. The two most common techniques are rotating managers on global assignments and communicating to suppliers the need for world-class performance and improvement.

2. Organize for global sourcing. This requires a restructuring to provide a cohesive management framework. The restructuring must create global commodity councils, total-cost decision-support systems, global purchasing offices, and global information systems. Global commodity groups facilitate the coordination and integration of different business units, global cost decision models are used to develop and share total cost information associated with different supply options, global purchasing offices effectively develop global supply knowledge, and global information systems collect information on global supply sources and market trends.

3. Configure a supply base. To achieve SCS, this must be a truly globalized supply base that leverages supplier

capabilities all over the world successfully. The suppliers in this base can supply any location worldwide, with competitive pricing, quality, delivery, and technology performance.

4. Develop supplier capabilities. This is done not by telling a supplier to improve, but actually using a hands-on approach to helping partners achieve performance improvement.

Such strategies have No Boundaries. Thanks to the Internet and real-time communications, the geographic location of source materials, manufacturing plants, value-added processing, storage, and distribution is no longer relevant. The issue becomes elapsed time-to-market, response to demand creation, and sustainable value creation. In other words, the location of an item is less important than knowing when it will be available.

CONCLUSION

The underlying theme of SCS is No Boundaries. The global implication of this is enormous, because SCS is not only about No Boundaries between links and partners—it is also about No Boundaries (or borders) between geographical locations. SCS views the world holistically and therefore it is the best strategy for achieving success in today's global economy.

17

THE SCS SUCCESS PATH FORWARD

"A road to a world with no borders, no boundaries, no flags, no countries."
—Carlos Santana, Grammy Award Winner

SCS is the best kind of journey—one that takes you into the future. After all, a journey backward into the past only happens in fiction, and SCS is not fiction. SCS is real. Although we live in the present, to achieve SCS, we must always be thinking about the future. This does not refer only to the near future, but to the distant future as well. It is the same as Peak-to-Peak Performance: We should not be looking at the next peak—we should be looking at the next, next peak and the peak after that and the peak after that, and so on.

Those who wish to achieve SCS cannot rely on the methods of the past for success. SCS means breaking new ground and forging the SCS Success Path Forward with No Boundaries as you pursue the journey. This is not to say that you make SCS up as you go along—there is a definite plan to follow. However, it is likely that the plan you follow will forge a path that has not been forged before.

Those of you who have reached this part of the book by reading all the way through may be a bit puzzled at this point because you are remembering that SCS is a continuous improvement process. As such, parts of SCS will be revisited often. So, you may be wondering if that is a path backward. Let me put your minds at rest: It is not. Each time a process is improved, it is not the same process—it is only the same type of process. So you may lay the same type of stone or brick down as you've laid before, but it is now in a different and new place.

The plan for an SCS Success Path forward has the following steps:

- Establish an SCS Steering Team.
- Conduct an SCS benchmark assessment.
- Develop a business plan.
- Conduct Customer and Supplier Roundtables.
- Conduct Leadership Roundtables.
- Define SCS Vision and Evidence of Success.
- Define prioritized SCS opportunities for improvement.
- Establish SCS Communications Team.
- Establish SCS Improvement Teams.
- Implement SCS Improvement Teams' Recommendations.
- Assess Evidence of Success.
- Define new prioritized opportunities for improvement.

This chapter will examine these steps, defining them where necessary and using examples where appropriate, so that you may use them in your own plan for an SCS Success Path Forward.

ESTABLISH SCS STEERING TEAM

The SCS Steering Team is the team that will be defining the direction the supply chain will be taking to achieve SCS. This team should be created from the top level of the supply chain partners' organizations, ideally, the top leaders from each supply chain partner should comprise the team. Because the SCS Steering Team will be responsible for driving the supply chain toward SCS, its members must have a clear understanding of SCS, knowledge of the role(s) of each partner in the supply chain, good insight and foresight, and a healthy imagination.

The purpose of the SCS Steering Team is to establish, communicate, and maintain focus on SCS and to develop the SCS business plan, vision, and evidence of success. SCS Steering Team members should individually and collectively demonstrate this focus. They must also demonstrate a united commitment to BPCI and the process of Revolution. Their first action should be to develop a charter. This charter should include the team's scope, the problem-solving and decision-making processes for the team, quantitative measures for the team and their deadlines, team resources, team budget, constraints, and authority. All members should be aligned and should understand the team charter, as it will serve as a guiding document for the team. There should be regularly scheduled meetings for SCS Steering Team business and periodic checks to make sure that commitment to the charter and SCS continues to run high.

CONDUCT AN SCS BENCHMARK ASSESSMENT

An SCS benchmark assessment is a critical examination of how SCS is viewed by all partners and by the ultimate customer and is therefore a measure of the health of the supply chain in question. A successful method for conducting the SCS Benchmark Assessment is a nine-point audit that examines

1. The progress made throughout the supply chain with SCS
2. How equipped supply chain partners are to handle change
3. How well supply chain partners understand Peak-to-Peak Performance
4. How well supply chain partners understand and apply a Total Operations philosophy
5. If supply chain partners are striving for customer satisfaction
6. If supply chain partners are practicing SCS manufacturing
7. If supply chain partners are practicing distribution synthesis
8. How well supply chain partners understand SCS partnerships
9. How well supply chain partners understand SCS communications.

After assessing each point, the next step is to assess the total scope of the supply chain operations as well. This is done by compiling scores based on each audit point and then studying them. This assessment will play a key role in the prioritization step. Appendix B is an example of an SCS benchmark assessment.

DEVELOP A BUSINESS PLAN

The SCS Steering Team is responsible for developing an SCS business plan. This should be a multi-year, macro-level business plan that will serve as the requirements definition for the future of the supply chain. It, therefore, should be a set of goals and performance measures to assure that all partners have a common view of the path forward. This will help the SCS Steering Team and other leaders stay focused on SCS. It also will help prepare them for changes in the supply chain and SCS requirements.

CONDUCT CUSTOMER AND SUPPLIER ROUNDTABLES

The term "roundtable" has several definitions. The definition that best suits SCS is "a meeting of peers for discussion and exchange of views." Customer and Supplier Roundtables should be include representatives from those suppliers all along the supply chain, as well as the ultimate consumer. The purpose of the roundtables is to provide a facilitated opportunity for suppliers and customers to share ideas about products and markets interactively, query existing beliefs, and uncover new opinions.

The information collected from a Customer and Supplier Roundtable provides unique input into the development of a strategic plan for SCS. The relationships they foster between customers and suppliers are invaluable as supply chain partners strive to achieve SCS. For example, participants are more clearly exposed to the complexity of supply chain relationships and become more confident as together they develop solutions from the roundtable questioning process.

Customer and Supplier Roundtables should be conducted on a regular basis so that supply chain members and the SCS Steering Team are aware of changes in the supply chain. They also need to be regular and ongoing; as each roundtable prepares follow-up questions, the answers to these questions must be addressed to elicit even deeper understanding of the future.

CONDUCT LEADERSHIP ROUNDTABLES

Leadership Roundtables work under the premise of intellectual power. When used with the process of strategic planning, they can be a highly successful tool. However, like other means of gathering data and assessing it so that conclusions may be drawn, a Leadership Roundtable requires a high degree of skill, experience, and technical competence. A successful roundtable session uncovers data that will benefit all planning processes, including that of the multi-year business plan.

The participants in Leadership Roundtables should have an interest in and a knowledge of a given part of the supply chain. They should also be leaders in their respective organizations. To capitalize on Leadership Roundtable results, a consistent methodology must be applied:

- The purpose must be clearly defined and understood.
- Participants must be present and ready to interact openly.
- A neutral setting and atmosphere of amnesty must exist.
- A carefully designed set of questions must be administered by the facilitator, who provides unbiased input to the strategic planning team.

DEFINE SCS VISION AND EVIDENCE OF SUCCESS

An SCS vision is not the doubletalk and doublethink so prevalent in American business today. Instead, it is the type of vision I defined in *Revolution*: "A description of where you are headed." The SCS vision should be stated so that the present is described as a past condition of the future, not as a future condition of the past. It should be expressions of optimism, hope, excellence, ideals, and possibilities for your supply chain for tomorrow. An example of an SCS vision for the automotive industry might be, "To be the world's best automotive supply chain by creating true partnerships with suppliers and customers, continuously improving customer satisfaction, using the best and most effective methods of technology communication, and harnessing the energy of change."

My recommendation for any SCS Steering Team that defines its vision is to create a robust Model of Success. As Warren Bennis, the author of *On Becoming a Leader,* said, "Action without vision is stumbling in the dark and vision without action is poverty-stricken poetry." In reality, a vision is only part of an entire Model of Success, which is comprised of:

1. Vision—a description of where you are headed
2. Mission—how to accomplish the Vision
3. Requirements of Success—the science of your business (or in the case of SCS, the science of your supply chain)
4. Guiding Principles—the values to practice while pursuing the vision
5. Evidence of Success—measurable results that will demonstrate when an organization (or supply chain) is moving towards the vision.

To define the Evidence of Success, those who defined the first four parts of the Model of Success must define the organizational entity to be measured, the perspective of measurement, and the performance to be measured. In the case of SCS, the organizational entity is the supply chain. The perspective of measurement could be partners, customers, and suppliers. The performance to be measured could be

- Supply chain health
- Supply chain effectiveness
- Supply chain efficiency
- Supply chain quality
- Supply chain partnerships
- Supply chain communications
- Supply chain financials.

It will be up to all supply chain partners to determine how these should be measured. One method would be to model the Evidence of Success along the lines of the SCS benchmark assessment.

DEFINE PRIORITIZED SCS OPPORTUNITIES FOR IMPROVEMENT

The SCS benchmark assessment is a very useful tool in defining SCS opportunities for improvement. For example, a client of ours has evaluated each of the core requirements for SCS based on its current operations. Its total evaluation reveals that target areas for improvement are customer satisfaction and manufacturing synthesis; the overall health of the supply chain, as a result, is poor as well. These target areas were determined when each criterion in the audit was investigated. A method for investigating each criterion is in Appendix B.

After determining of the core competencies of SCS, the organization focuses its continuous improvement efforts on the two areas listed above, using a Communications Team and Improvement Teams.

ESTABLISH SCS COMMUNICATION TEAM

The responsibility of the SCS Communication Team is to ensure and assure that everyone in the supply chain has a clear understanding of the SCS Model of Success, the status of teams, and the status of SCS. Like all teams, it should have a charter with the components I described in the section on the SCS Steering Team. All SCS teams need charters.

The Communications Team has many tools at its disposal for conveying these messages, but it must also keep in mind that these communications will travel across many organizations all over the world, so they must be familiar with electronic forms of communication. I also recommend that the SCS Communications Team schedule regular Communication Forums. These forums are essential to ensuring alignment, understanding, and celebration. Such a forum should consist of a review of the SCS Model of Success and team or partner presentations that cover the status of their role in SCS, questions about SCS, and challenges they may be facing. Since supply chain partners most likely will be in different geographical across the globe, it might be wise to investigate electronic ways of conducting these. No Boundaries to communication should separate them.

ESTABLISH SCS IMPROVEMENT TEAMS

The SCS Improvement Teams are where the process of SCS resides. For supply chain partners to achieve SCS, they must create and charter many SCS Improvement Teams all along the supply chain. These teams then will focus on incremental and continuous improvement in the areas defined in the process of prioritizing SCS opportunities for improvement. Some of these teams will be cross functional: They will address a specific improvement opportunity with representatives across the supply chain. Others may be functional and address improvements in the organization of a specific partner.

The members of the SCS Improvement Teams should be from broad cross-sections of the supply chain and should have demonstrated in the past that they are capable of achieving continuous improvements, breakthroughs, and innovation to enhance performance. The scope of each SCS Improvement Team charter should be consistent with the knowledge of the members on the team and of sufficient focus to allow the team to achieve real performance improvements. It is critical that these teams meet as often as necessary so that they may develop specific recommendations and plans of action to achieve peak performance in the areas that need improvement.

IMPLEMENT RECOMMENDATIONS OF THE SCS IMPROVEMENT TEAMS

The SCS Improvement Teams' recommendations are to be shared with the SCS Steering Team for review and approval. Once the Steering Team approves the recommendations, they should be implemented. Communicating the approved recommendations then becomes the task of the Communications Team. The SCS Steering Team should remain committed to implementing the recommendations throughout the implementation process.

ASSESS EVIDENCE OF SUCCESS

Those involved with the implementation of the Improvement Team recommendations and the SCS Steering Team should maintain an ongoing record that tracks performance against the defined Evidence of Success. The record should be reviewed periodically to prioritize the next opportunities for improvement. The Communications Team should disseminate information ongoing continuous improvements throughout the supply chain.

DEFINE NEW PRIORITIZED OPPORTUNITIES FOR IMPROVEMENT

Based on another SCS Benchmark Assessment conducted after the Evidence of Success shows that performance has improved, the SCS Steering Team should prioritize the opportunities for the next iteration of the SCS process. This is truly continuous improvement in action. Supply chain partners working toward the goal of SCS should never stop looking for ways to improve. They must lay down the same types of stones or bricks in the path again and again if they wish to keep moving forward.

CONCLUSION

Successful improvement implementations may not remain successful. SCS is a dynamic process; like the river I like to compare it to, it is always moving. That means supply chain members should move with it and continuous improvement efforts are the best way to keep up with the motion. The SCS journey of never-ending peak-to-peak evolution is the process that will provide your supply chain with the competitive advantage required to achieve sustained success.

18

SCS APPLICATIONS

"All successful men have agreed in one thing—they were causationists. They believed that things went not by luck, but by law; that there was not a weak or a cracked link in the chain that joins the first and last of things."

—Ralph Waldo Emerson

The pursuit of SCS nets real results. However, sometimes the results are different from what is expected. A recent experience with a client is a case in point. An analysis of our client's supply chain resulted in a series of opportunities for improvement. As we drilled down on these opportunities, it became clear that before we pursued SCS, we needed to address their links as there were boundaries between their plants that needed to be eliminated prior to their beginning to address SCS. As we began to drill down on the boundaries between the plants, we discovered an even more basic problem. There existed substantial boundaries between the departments within their plants. So, the priority was not to implement SCS, but rather to eliminate the boundaries between departments first and then tackle those between plants. Interestingly, eliminating the department and then the plant boundaries not only positioned us to begin SCS; it also netted considerable improvements in operational performance. So, the initial results from pursuing SCS were not supply chain results but rather department, plant, and then link results. From there, we moved on to the results that could be achieved at the supply chain level.

The SCS path forward requires both strategic and tactical initiatives. The strategic initiatives center on establishing objectives and implementing continuous improvement recommendations to achieve performance excellence. Tactical initiatives center on fixing problems and resolving issues that detract from operational excellence. So, both continuous improvement (strategic) and the problem solving (tactical) processes need to be addressed for departments, plants, links, and then the overall supply chain.

This chapter begins with a discussion of how to apply the SCS process and then illustrates this process with an overview of the efforts pursued for the situation just described.

APPLICATION OF THE SCS PROCESS

The focus of SCS is using innovation, integration, and implementation to create a strategic, responsive, and collaborative supply chain, with an emphasis on an increased ability to harness the energy of change. The results include

- Increased ROI
- Increased throughput, productivity, and speed
- Increased customer satisfaction
- Higher stakeholder value
- Increased profitability
- Improved return on assets through increased inventory turns
- Reduced total costs
- Increased market share through excellence in supply chain integration.

The SCS effort for the above-mentioned application where boundaries existed between departments and plants was broken into three parts: supply chain design, supply chain systems, and supply chain continuous improvement. These three were then applied strategically and tactically for the synthesized departments, plants, links, and chains. So, initiatives that needed pursuit were:

- Type 1—Strategic department design
- Type 2—Strategic plant design
- Type 3—Strategic link design
- Type 4—Strategic chain design
- Type 5—Strategic department system
- Type 6—Strategic plant systems
- Type 7—Strategic link systems
- Type 8—Strategic chain systems
- Type 9—Strategic department continuous improvement
- Type 10—Strategic plant continuous improvement
- Type 11—Strategic link continuous improvement
- Type 12—Strategic chain continuous improvement
- Type 13—Tactical department design
- Type 14—Tactical plant design
- Type 15—Tactical link design
- Type 16—Tactical chain design
- Type 17—Tactical department systems
- Type 18—Tactical plant systems
- Type 19—Tactical link systems
- Type 20—Tactical chain systems
- Type 21—Tactical department continuous improvement
- Type 22—Tactical plant continuous improvement
- Type 23—Tactical link continuous improvement
- Type 24—Tactical chain continuous improvement.

APPLICATION PRIORITIZATION

As an illustration of the SCS process, the preliminary prioritization of the efforts to be pursued for the previously described application were

1. A strategic link Model of Success (Type 3)—one that defines the five elements of a Model of Success: Vision, Mission, Requirements of Success, Guiding Principles, and Evidence of Success. This Model of Success was not for the chain but rather for the link so that the link could be integrated as preparation for later pursuing SCS.

DEVELOPING A LINK MODEL OF SUCCESS AND ACHIEVING ALIGNMENT

A powerful and transforming link Model of Success must answer five questions:

1. Where is our link headed?
2. How will our link get there?
3. What is the science of our business?
4. What values will we practice within our link?
5. How will we measure the success of our link?

The answers to these questions will define the five elements of the link Model of Success: Vision, Mission, Requirements of Success, Guiding Principles, and Evidence of Success.

After the Model of Success has been created, the next step is to achieve alignment, or "buy-in." The alignment must be not only within one plant of our link, but across all links. The eight "Ps" of facilitating alignment are

1. Precedence: alignment must be preceded by the creation of the Model of Success.
2. Public: the Model of Success must be communicated publicly. This cannot be a one-time communication; it must be pervasive, persistent, and ongoing.
3. Personal: alignment is best achieved when it is not limited. The personalities of each individual or supply chain involved in the alignment process must be considered and taken into account.
4. Practical: a real, viable, and practical set of reasons for the Model of Success must be developed and communicated.
5. Progressive: a Model of Success is never finished. It requires a process that must be nurtured over time, as does alignment.

> 6. Pledge-based: no one can force alignment on someone else. It involves a personal decision of enrollment.
>
> 7. Powerful: alignment provides a powerful focus because it is a high level of commitment and loyalty.
>
> 8. Persistent: parts of alignment require a lot of effort on the part of supply chain leaders, particularly persistence. Alignment requires persistent, consistent repetition of the same thoughts, ideas, and concepts from leaders.

2. A tactical continuous improvement effort of rationalization at the link level (Type 23)—this begins with a systematic examination of processes, products and inventory, and suppliers. In this application there were hundreds of products, thousands of business processes, and hundreds of vendors; streamlining them all was the goal. The questions asked included:

   - Why are we making this product? Do we need to continue making it? What is the value-add?
   - Why do we have this manufacturing process? Can we improve it or eliminate it?
   - Why are we using this vendor? Is this vendor's product or system necessary? What is the value-add?

   Asking questions like these provided answers that were useful in eliminating wasteful processes and practices, as well as reengineering others for efficiency and effectiveness.

3. A strategic global network design at the chain level (Type 4)—to assure the correct links are in the correct locations to support the evolution of SCS.

GLOBAL NETWORK DESIGN

In a global network, all organizations and operations must be integrated. Integration of these organizations and operations may be achieved in six steps:

1. Confirm that the requirements of your supply chain over the planning horizon
2. Define interface standards. These standards should include operational, procedural, IT, organizational, and measurement standards.
3. Define alternative global networks
4. Evaluate alternative global networks
5. Establish a global network path forward
6. Define implementation plan and obtain leadership buy-in.

4. A strategic systems effort focused on the procurement process at the link level (Type 7)—the strategic procurement process is the procurement process that obtains the best-quality, low-cost parts, and materials availability. For this application, the current procurement practices had to be assessed to assure that they were indeed obtaining those parts and materials and when they were not, determining methods for doing so that were efficient, streamlined, and cost-effective.

5. A strategic design effort focused on operational centralization at the link level (Type 3)—this priority involved a global view of the link's operations with a view to integrating all the link functions so that operations were not duplicated and departments that perform the same task were merged.

6. A strategic design initiative of manufacturing synthesis at the plant level (Type 2)—this synthesis involved the elimination of a push methodology and the implementation of a push to a generic product level, as well as customization on demand.

7. A tactical initiative of forecasting planning and process improvement at the chain level (Type 20)—this effort required the elimination of boundaries and the sharing of information throughout the chain to improve the visibility of requirements.

8. A tactical effort focused on inventory planning and management at the chain level (Type 20)—this effort required the integration of the process used to plan production based upon chain requirements.

9. A tactical initiative of transportation planning and management at the chain level (Type 16)—this effort involved a review of current transportation methods across the chain and the reduction of costs and increase of service for the chain as presently configured.

10. A tactical initiative of assembly and manufacturing layout at the plant level (Type 14)—this effort required the assessment and improvement of the manufacturing processes and layout based on Winning Manufacturing and manufacturing synthesis.

11. A tactical initiative of vendor rationalization at the chain level (Type 13)— this effort required scrutinizing all vendors to provide a clear rationale for why they vendors are necessary in the supply chain, with a view to eliminating unnecessary vendors, waste, and vendor costs.

12. A tactical initiative of vendor-managed inventory at the chain level (Type 16)—this effort involved the pursuit of a system where the order cycle was reduced and the vendor defined the reorder point for the customer order cycle and then triggered the fulfillment of that order. The vendor captured the activity from the point of manufacture and computed the amount of product required for replenishment.

13. A tactical design effort focused on implementing warehousing operational best practices at the plant level (Type 14)—the warehousing operational best practices are those that achieve warehousing operational excellence through distribution synthesis. This effort involved the improvement of the receiving, storing, picking, and

shipping functions to achieve best practices for the current operation.

14. A strategic communications design initiative at the chain level (Type 8)—this effort included the design of Web-based communications and visibility systems so as to guide the evolution of the communications system in accordance with the strategic direction.

15. A strategic systems initiative of order management software with global visibility at the plant level (Type 6)—the development of the order management software that takes orders and determines inventory availability on a global basis to complete the planning side of the systems equation.

16. A tactical systems initiative looking at order flow at the plant level (Type 18)—this effort addressed the order flow from when an order comes into a plant until it is filled. The need was to simplify the process and to assure responsiveness.

17. A tactical systems initiative of leveraging planning methods at the plant level (Type 18)—the standardization of the effective use of the planning methods already in place at the plant level and the addition of new or different methods as required.

18. A tactical systems initiative of aligning software and update deadlines at the plant level (Type 18)—due to a wide diversity of non-integrated software packages at the plant level, this effort involved the aligning of software upgrades and the coordination of schedules to assure a minimum of disruption and cost was to be incurred.

19. A strategic continuous improvement initiative at the plant level (Type 10)—an application of the BPCI process for each plant. This involved the identification of plant operating performance and the improvement of these performance measures via BPCI.

20. A strategic design initiative of concurrent engineering at the plant level (Type 2)—the redesign of organizational structures, systems, and procedures to increase speed and reduce costs of new product introduction.

21. A tactical department design initiative (Type 13)—this effort focused on organizational structures, equipment, space, staff, systems, and layout of each department and the identification of opportunities for improvement.

22. A strategic design initiative of training at the link level— (Type 3) this effort addressed the link's supply chain training requirements by adhering to the following elements of training:

   A. Training must be done Just-in-Time: *Uncover* the need for knowledge, *discover* new knowledge, and *recover* by putting new knowledge into action.

   B. Training must be part of the process of creating Peak-To-Peak Performance and therefore aligned with the link's vision of SCS, using the link's teaming vocabulary, culture, and process.

   C. Training must be flexible. In other words, individual needs must be assessed and the training customized to meet them.

   D. Training must have full leadership support at all levels. This support should be proactive to maximize training awards.

   E. Training must be presented in short, interactive sessions by high-quality, well-prepared, and interesting people.

   F. Training must be built into the schedule and not so that people are behind on their functions upon a return from training.

   G. Training must be accountable. It is important to conduct follow-up testing, probing, and measuring of all training. Employees should be recognized for the successful completion of training.

   H. Teams should be the focus of training.

   I. Training must be viewed as a priority.

   J. Training objectives must be focused. The facilitator and all training session attendees must understand what they will learn from the training and they must then be able to state why it is important to them.

23. A tactical continuous improvement initiative of customer satisfaction at the link level (Type 23)—a customer satisfaction process was put in place to define the customer, define what the customer wants, identify present performance, and identify how to increase customer satisfaction.

24. A tactical continuous improvement initiative of performance metrics at the link level (Type 23)—there are various performance metrics that can be used to establish a baseline of link performance. This effort identified the most meaningful performance metrics and established the performance levels against which to judge performance.

25. A tactical continuous improvement initiative of production scheduling at the plant level (Type 22)—this effort involved the plant scheduling to meet the link requirements. Different plants utilized different processes and different scheduling tools. This effort selected the best processes and tools and standardized them across all plants.

CONCLUSION

Supply chain results take place as a result of strategic and tactical initiatives at the department, plant, link, and chain levels for design, systems, and continuous improvement. This is the reality of SCS and illustrates how you need to push forward to achieve SCS excellence.

19

CONCLUSION

"The horizon leans forward, offering you space to place new steps of change."

—Maya Angelou

SCS is not a quick fix—it is a continuous process. IT is its enabler, but people are the key to leveraging technology and harnessing the energy of change. Because SCS involves people and it asks that those people change their behavior and attitudes, SCS takes time. SCS also takes patience and perseverance—and a Revolution. You and your organization can create this Revolution. The tools are there and they are not difficult to master. The main things to keep in mind are

- SCS is Beyond SCM
- SCS will result in major organizational success
- SCS is the path forward
- "When you come to a fork in the road.... Take it!"
  – Yogi Berra.

SCS can truly be done. You can ensure that there are No Boundaries in your supply chain. Choose a direction and begin the journey. Think of the people you'll meet on the way and consider how you can convince them to join you on this journey. And as Mr. Berra advises, take that fork in the road. You'll be glad you did and so will they.

GO! GO! GO!

Appendix A
Winning Manufacturing—
The 20 Requirements of
Success

1. **Manufacturing Costs:** Manufacturing costs must be significantly reduced. Winning manufacturing requires manufacturing cost reductions of 40 to 60 percent This should be achieved through quality leadership that raises the expectations and aspirations of the organization, defines manufacturing costs precisely and accurately, sets specific cost reduction goals, and audits implemented performance to anticipated performance.

2. **Manufacturing and Marketing:** Manufacturing and marketing must become integrated and function as a team. Winning manufacturing cannot be achieved at the expense of another team player. Marketing and manufacturing must call a truce mandated by upper management. Then, manufacturing and marketing must use communication to achieve peace and an ongoing, long-term commitment to work in unison through the understanding that their individual successes are tied to mutual success. After peace is achieved, the goal is synergy,

which takes manufacturing and marketing beyond working together to true integration.

3. **Product Development:** Product development must become an integrated, iterative process. Product development is the interactive process whereby the customer, marketing, sales, product designers, process designers, purchasing, vendors, and manufacturing work together to develop a product that meets customer expectations and can be manufactured economically. It should be integrated on a product-by-product basis; the product team should be broad-based; the customers' needs and wants should be known to the entire team; the product team should include members from marketing, sales, product designers, process designers, purchasing, manufacturing, and vendors; and the product team should live with the product from preliminary design through successful production.

4. **Global Marketplace:** All manufacturing decisions must be made within the context of an integrated global strategy. The first step is to assess current status. The second step is to establish a series of global goals, along with a variety of approaches that can help achieve these goals. After that, the best global strategy should be identified, sold to management, implemented, and audited. A team should also be given the task of maintaining a watch on the global horizon and this team should participate in all Winning Manufacturing deliberations.

5. **Lead Times:** Significant reductions in lead times must occur. The methods of doing business must be changed to reduce lead times significantly. This cannot be done by working faster, but must be done by reducing production lead time. *Winning Manufacturing* has a clearly defined procedure for reducing lot times, which includes documenting present customer lead time, analyzing the competition, establishing a goal, identifying bottlenecks, and creating multi-department teams.

6. **Production Lot Sizes:** Production for lot sizes and setup times must be reduced. This is a nine-step procedure that calls for documenting present lot sizes, identifying specific lot sizes for reduction, reducing setup times through lean manufacturing, calculating economic lot size, identifying alternative methods for efficient material handling, justifying the investment required to accomplish reduction, defining and obtaining support for specific improvement plans, implementing the reduced setup time and material handling equipment as justified, and beginning production of reduced lot sizes.

7. **Uncertainty:** All uncertainty must be minimized: discipline must be increased. All manufacturing activities must have clear, well-established standards, and all activities must conform to these standards to reduce uncertainty. This requires balance, focus, and continuous flow.

8. **Balance:** All manufacturing operations must be balanced. This means determining the cycle time that must be met to satisfy production requirements and pacing all manufacturing processes to this cycle time.

9. **Production and Inventory Control:** The production and inventory control system must be straightforward and transparent. Straightforward production and inventory control systems are systems that are easily understood. Transparent ones are logical and intuitive. To control production and inventory in Winning Manufacturing, several steps must be undertaken in a straightforward and transparent manner. These are defining the products, families, and options to be produced; defining the volume of products, families, and options to be produced; specifying a production plan; determining when materials and capacity should be present to meet the production plan; scheduling material delivery from vendors; scheduling focused factories; and monitoring schedule adherence.

10. **Inventory:** Drastic reductions in inventory must occur. This begins by documenting present levels of inventory and

comparing them to whatever industry yardsticks can be obtained. Specific goals should be established, an audit conducted, and specific approaches to reduce inventory should be considered to certify that inventory, as well as the total costs of manufacturing, will be reduced. Once the most justifiable approaches have been chosen, then they must be integrated into an overall plan and the results should be compared to established goals. Procedures must also be in place that will assure continued conformance to the goals.

11. **Adaptability:** Manufacturing facilities, operations, and personnel must become more adaptable. This means flexibility (which requires focused factories, small product lot sizes, versatile equipment, and multiskilled employees) and modularity (which requires modular facilities, modular focused departments, and use of time modularity). Fixed rules or methods for achieving adaptable manufacturing do not exist. The level of flexibility and modularity that is appropriate for one operation may not be appropriate for another and can only be determined by applying judgment and experience.

12. **Quality:** Product quality, vendor quality, and information quality must improve. A successful quality improvement program should be a broad-based, participative effort involving upper management, middle management, purchasing, product development, engineering, marketing, supervision, shop-floor personnel, vendors, and customers. Everyone who has an impact on quality must be educated to obtain an awareness and understanding of quality.

13. **Maintenance:** Manufacturing process failures must be minimized. Reliability must be maximized. Winning Manufacturing operations cannot tolerate manufacturing process failures. To minimize such failures, maintenance must become an important management priority. The following must also be pursued: redundancy, modularity, obsolescence, maintenance personnel, maintenance training and education, expert systems, working environment, mainte-

nance management, maintenance database, maintenance storeroom, maintenance inventory, maintenance and engineering, and maintenance profession.

14. **Material Flow:** Material flow must be efficient. Before designing a Winning Manufacturing material handling system, you must have established winning material flow requirements by reducing lead times, production lots, and inventory, and established focused departments and focused factories. Then, the material handling system should be designed by pursuing the following steps: defining the system's objectives and scope, establishing material flow requirements, generating alternative designs for meeting material flow requirements, evaluating alternative designs, selecting the preferred design, establishing an improvement plan, obtaining support for the plan, implementing the preferred system, and auditing systems performance and refining as necessary.

15. **Material Tracking and Control:** Material tracking and control systems must be upgraded. Responsive, continuous-flow manufacturing cannot function without upgraded material tracking and control systems and Winning Manufacturing cannot be achieved. A material tracking and control team should be established to work in unison with the Winning Manufacturing team to define the overall approach to material tracking and control, and the overall computer system architecture. Then, after working to create a material tracking and control system design, the team should upgrade the material tracking and control systems.

16. **Human Resources:** Every manager must be dedicated to creating an environment where every employee is motivated and happy. The company should hire employees that believe they are winners and then make sure that winners remain winners. The two most critical components of creating this environment are employee development and trust.

17. **Team Players:** Everyone associated with manufacturing must work together as a team. For Winning Manufacturing,

the characteristics of a successful team are shared vision, shared values, shared expectations, shared commitment, shared confidence, shared responsibility, and shared rewards. A methodical teaming process must be utilized to drive continuous improvement.

18. **Simplification:** All of manufacturing must be simplified. This means streamlining and simplifying manufacturing in four areas: product design, manufacturing processes, organizational structure, and operating systems. Simplified product design has two consistent characteristics: the reduction of number of parts in a product and the use of standard parts. Simplified organizational structure means simplifying communications and lines of authority and minimizing the number of layers in the organization. Simplified manufacturing processes are achieved through 12 Requirements of Success:

   - Simplified product design
   - Reduced lead time
   - Reduced production lot sizes
   - Reduced uncertainty
   - Balanced, focused departments and factories
   - Straightforward and transparent production and inventory control systems
   - Reduced inventories
   - Increased adaptability
   - Increased quality
   - Reduced down times
   - Continuous-flow manufacturing
   - Upgraded tracking and control systems.

19. **Integration:** All organizations and operations must be integrated. The two prerequisites of Winning Manufacturing integration are dynamic consistency and interface standards. The steps in the process of integrating operations and organizations are these: to confirm that the 20 Requirements of Success are your company's vision of where your organization is heading; define interface standards; pursue specific

Requirements of Success; implement improvements for the specific Requirements of Success that were pursued; integrate improved operations with ongoing improved operations; continue to pursue improvements; and continue to pursue Winning Manufacturing.

20. **Understanding:** Manufacturing management must understand Winning Manufacturing, particularly the two prerequisites of Winning Manufacturing: a commitment to winning and technical intimacy. Manufacturing management must reject fads, gimmicks, and quick fixes; fire fighting and short-term optimization; incremental analysis; and petty politics and adversarial relations. The process of understanding begins with an awareness of Winning Manufacturing and evolves as a Winning Manufacturing pioneer that leads manufacturing management to a commitment to Winning Manufacturing.

APPENDIX B
SCS BENCHMARK
ASSESSMENT

The following nine tables represent a version of an assessment tool to conduct the nine-point audit of the Supply Chain Benchmark Assessment.

FIRST AUDIT POINT OF SCS—SUPPLY CHAIN HEALTH

Action Item	1=Strongly Disagree		3=Agree		5=Strongly Agree
The supply chain process in the organization is well-defined and understood by all members of the supply chain.	1	2	3	4	5
There is not pervasive siloism within the supply chain; that is, supply chain members do not focus on self-optimization rather than optimization of the whole.	1	2	3	4	5
All supply chain links focus on customer satisfaction.	1	2	3	4	5
Information delays are not tolerated.	1	2	3	4	5
All supply chain members understand that change cannot be managed, only harnessed.	1	2	3	4	5
The supply chain has true and open partnerships that share information readily and expeditiously.	1	2	3	4	5
The competitive advantage of the entire pipeline is more important than the competitive advantage of each member of the pipeline.	1	2	3	4	5

Total Score This Section: _____

SECOND AUDIT POINT OF SCS—CHANGE

Action Item	1=Strongly Disagree		3=Agree		5=Strongly Agree
Each employee has clearly defined responsibilities, accountabilities, roles, and identities.	1	2	3	4	5
There is continuity in the purpose of the organization.	1	2	3	4	5
Expectations of each employee are delineated and only altered after conference and mutual agreement.	1	2	3	4	5
Everyone understands the necessity of change.	1	2	3	4	5
All employees believe that change will benefit them both personally and professionally.	1	2	3	4	5
The focus of employees within the organization is consistent with the focus of the organization itself.	1	2	3	4	5
Organizational focus is proactively, rather than reactively, maintained.	1	2	3	4	5
Employees are encouraged to participate in and provide feedback to organizational changes.	1	2	3	4	5
Information flows through the organization in a timely manner.	1	2	3	4	5

Total Score This Section: _____

THIRD AUDIT POINT OF SCS—PEAK-TO-PEAK PERFORMANCE

Action Item	1=Strongly Disagree		3=Agree		5=Strongly Agree
Peak performance is often the beginning of failure.	1	2	3	4	5
The organization is striving to evolve from a succeed/fail organization to a succeed/succeed one.	1	2	3	4	5
The organization needs to install processes that anticipate and solve problems before they are problems.	1	2	3	4	5
Continuous renewal is important in Peak-to-Peak Performance.	1	2	3	4	5
There will always be more problems than solutions.	1	2	3	4	5
The organization needs to solve problems by thinking "outside the box" and reaching to a level that is beyond the problem.	1	2	3	4	5
A shift to a process of continuously changing paths is required for Peak-to-Peak Performance.	1	2	3	4	5
Success only buys a ticket to higher-level problems.	1	2	3	4	5

Total Score This Section: _____

FOURTH AUDIT POINT OF SCS—TOTAL OPERATIONS

Action Item	1=Strongly Disagree		3=Agree		5=Strongly Agree
The correct distribution network and logistics methods are in place to provide product at the right place at the right time in the most cost-effective manner.	1	2	3	4	5
Operational efficiency is assured through the correct manufacturing and warehousing methods, resources, and processes.	1	2	3	4	5
Proper procedures are in place to protect against equipment breakdown and malfunction.	1	2	3	4	5
The quality control system provides the organization with tools necessary to reduce and even eliminate defects from our products.	1	2	3	4	5
There is adequate buffer to allow interruptions in service.	1	2	3	4	5
There is a process to assure continuous improvement in our operations.	1	2	3	4	5
There is a process to assure continuous improvement in our pipeline (i.e. partnerships and alliances).	1	2	3	4	5
The organization takes advantage of SCS and Total Operations to capture the energy of change.	1	2	3	4	5

Total Score This Section: _____

243

FIFTH AUDIT POINT OF SCS—CUSTOMER SATISFACTION

Action Item	1=Strongly Disagree		3=Agree		5=Strongly Agree
The organization believes that de-massification of product, rather than mass production, will be a driver of exemplary customer satisfaction.	1	2	3	4	5
The customer is the co-creator of value.	1	2	3	4	5
Ongoing customer dialogue is key to success.	1	2	3	4	5
Sharing of minds and wallets is more important than retention.	1	2	3	4	5
My organization is finding that sales and service are merging.	1	2	3	4	5
It is good business to treat customers as individuals rather than as demographics.	1	2	3	4	5
Customer segmentation based on order quantities and % of profit is a route to SCS.	1	2	3	4	5
Customer satisfaction issues impact more than product quality and service.	1	2	3	4	5

Total Score This Section: _____

SIXTH AUDIT POINT OF SCS—MANUFACTURING SYNTHESIS

Action Item	1=Strongly Disagree		3=Agree		5=Strongly Agree
Leadership understands that significant lead time reduction must occur.	1	2	3	4	5
The only way to maintain manufacturing efficiency while reducing production lot sizes is to reduce setup times.	1	2	3	4	5
The organization realizes that balancing a series of operations is more important than the speed of any of those operations.	1	2	3	4	5
The facility consists of focused departments that provide balance and support for manufacturing.	1	2	3	4	5
No one in manufacturing over- or under-produces.	1	2	3	4	5
WIP buffers are installed only when sequential flow cannot be achieved.	1	2	3	4	5
All uncertainty is minimized in manufacturing, and discipline increased since there is insufficient time to deal with unplanned and untimely events.	1	2	3	4	5
All operations are performed according to communicated, well-defined standards.	1	2	3	4	5

Total Score This Section: _____

SEVENTH AUDIT POINT OF SCS—DISTRIBUTION SYNTHESIS

Action Item	1=Strongly Disagree		3=Agree		5=Strongly Agree
The organization understands the importance of customer requirements and satisfaction when designing a distribution network.	1	2	3	4	5
Third party logistics (3PL) providers are often used in peak demand times to improve financial performance (i.e. replace seasonally utilized DCs).	1	2	3	4	5
The company has a Distribution Strategic Master Plan (DSMP), which defines the requirements for an efficient and effective distribution system.	1	2	3	4	5
The organization uses Leadership Round-tables early in the design of a distribution network to develop ideas about new products, customer requirements, technologies, and sourcing of materials.	1	2	3	4	5
All distribution decisions (e.g., number and location of DCs, inventory levels, optimal order cycles and fulfillment rates, and order procedures) are based in a SCS, rather than SCM (or even traditional logistics), environment.	1	2	3	4	5
Forecasting is not used in determining distribution requirements.	1	2	3	4	5
The organization uses a hybrid system of distribution to maximize customer satisfaction and optimize manufacturing efficiency.	1	2	3	4	5
Before any distribution network decisions are made, all viable alternatives are economically and qualitatively evaluated based on specific, weighted criteria.	1	2	3	4	5

Total Score This Section: _____

EIGHTH AUDIT POINT OF SCS—PARTNERSHIPS

Action Item	1=Strongly Disagree		3=Agree		5=Strongly Agree
The organization believes that the challenges one faces in partnerships (e.g. trust, communications, and culture) must be overcome to secure competitive advantage.	1	2	3	4	5
Improved performance of the TOTAL pipeline is necessary through partnerships.	1	2	3	4	5
The keys to partnership success are: integration, information, and interaction.	1	2	3	4	5
The organization is communicating with supply chain members on causes of problems, corrections, and continuous improvement, rather than on the problems themselves.	1	2	3	4	5
The days of "carrot and stick" vendor relationships are over.	1	2	3	4	5
The organization understands the importance of sharing information on sales and purchasing trends with its supply chain.	1	2	3	4	5
The organization chooses its partners based on both quantitative and qualitative criteria that specifically address strategic needs.	1	2	3	4	5
It is important to benchmark partnership activity for continuous improvement.	1	2	3	4	5

Total Score This Section: _____

NINTH AUDIT POINT OF SCS—COMMUNICATIONS

Action Item	1=Strongly Disagree		3=Agree		5=Strongly Agree
Managing and communicating information to supply chain partners is vital to organizational success.	1	2	3	4	5
Information and communications systems are different entities.	1	2	3	4	5
The organization's communications systems enable sharing of a wide variety of information forms.	1	2	3	4	5
The future of the supply chain communications systems is "e."	1	2	3	4	5
The organization is investing in technologies that facilitate information sharing through secure means.	1	2	3	4	5
All supply chain members use a variety of strategic, tactical, and technical information systems.	1	2	3	4	5
A homegrown legacy system is not the best example of how information can be shared through SCS communications.	1	2	3	4	5
The organization is comfortable with sharing enterprise information with its partners.	1	2	3	4	5

Total Score This Section: _____

EVALUATING CURRENT OPERATIONS

After assessing each of the elements of SCS, you should assess the total scope of your operations as well. Write down the figures for each of the nine areas in the spaces provided below.

	Rating	Target Rating
Supply Chain "Health"		35
Change		45
Peak-to-Peak		40
Total Operations		40
Customer Satisfaction		40
Manufacturing Synthesis		40
Distribution Synthesis		40
Partnerships		40
Communications		40
TOTAL		360

Rating ÷ Target Rating = _____%

A+	Excellent	97% and higher
A	Very Good	90 – 96.99%
B	Good	80 – 89.99%
C	Average	75 – 79.99%
C-	Below Average	70 – 74.99%
D	Poor	Less than 70%

For example, Forsyth Widgets, Inc. has evaluated each of the core requirements for SCS based on its current operations. Its total evaluation, when placed in table form, reveals the following:

	Rating	Target Rating
Supply Chain "Health"	24	35
Change	37	45
Peak-to-Peak	28	40
Total Operations	32	40
Customer Satisfaction	25	40
Manufacturing Synthesis	21	40
Distribution Synthesis	27	40
Partnerships	34	40
Communications	27	40
TOTAL	255	360

A score of 255/360 = 71%, or C- (below average). This should be an indicator to the company that many areas of SCS require responsive and comprehensive re-envisioning; success within the supply chain cannot happen otherwise. The next step should be investigating each criterion and determining specific courses of action.

AUDIT ITEMS COMPARED

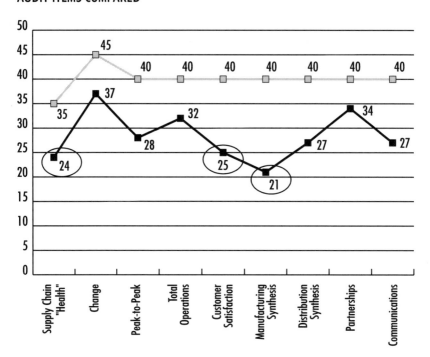

Appendix C
Glossary of Terms

↗ . The whitewater we live in is symbolized by an arrow that turns upward at a 90-degree angle. This is in comparison to the many eras before now where Change was relaxed and gradual.

Adaptability. The ability to adjust to sudden shifts in volume.

Agile manufacturing. One step beyond lean manufacturing; based on the principles of delivering value to the customer, being responsive to change, valuing human knowledge and skills, and forming virtual partnerships.

Approach. A one-time implementation of a methodology with the expectation of immediate results.

Asset-based 3PL. Offer dedicated logistics services through use of their expanded assets.

Blurred boundaries. When distribution and manufacturing take on the functions of each other to streamline time–to–market, to customize products at the last minute, and to increase customer satisfaction.

Build to Order (BTO). The philosophy that each customer requires specific and unique value-adds to products in order to derive the most from them.

Business Process Continuous Improvement (BPCI). A leadership-driven process that uses teams and a Model of Success to alter company culture and organizational operating style.

Cellular Manufacturing. Helps companies reduce WIP through the use of Group Technology principles, which provide a methodology for designing cells that produce families of parts.

Change. Constant whitewater and lack of steady state; a core competency of SCS.

Change Management. A misnomer; the energy of change can be harnessed but never managed.

Collaborative Planning, Forecasting, and Replenishment (CPFR). Enables real-time, open and secure communications and supports a broad set of requirements while allowing customers to contribute to the generation of numbers and participate in other parts of the process to improve accuracy.

Consolidation. The unification of businesses, divisions, and functions to eliminate duplication and create additional competitive strength and visibility.

Consortium. When similar companies in the same kind of business band together to pool their resources to conduct research, evaluate technology, or lobby for a political position.

Constraints-based. In manufacturing: the reference to "bottlenecks" in the system that delay production.

Contingency Planning. Considering the "what if's" that might happen in business and planning for their challenges before they become realities.

Core Competencies. The eight ways to meet the challenges of business today and achieve SCS are to understand: change, peak-to-peak performance, customer satisfaction, Total Operations, manufacturing synthesis, distribution synthesis, partnerships, and communications.

Crossdocking. Moving received goods directly to outbound shipping, eliminating storage and orderpicking altogether.

Customer Satisfaction. The difference between the customer's expectation of service and the customer's perception of the service received; a core competency of SCS.

Customer Satisfaction Design. Developing an across-the-chain strategy for meeting customer requirements, being responsive to changing customer needs, and identifying information and other technology requirements that will improve process control and productivity.

Delaying. The creation of a custom product at the last minute.

Deverticalization. The process of eliminating segments of a business, either through outsourcing or sale, that are not core competencies in order to focus on the elements that are.

Distribution Requirements Planning (DRP). The application of Manufacturing Requirements Planning (MRP) to the distribution environment; a dynamic model that examines a time-based plan of events that affect inventory.

Distribution Strategic Master Plan (DSMP). A process for applying strategic planning to distribution processes.

Distribution Synthesis. Tailoring a distribution solution that maximizes customer satisfaction; finding a balance between push and pull methods of distribution; a core competency of SCS.

e-SCS. The transaction of business through the Internet or other virtual means (e.g., Electronic Data Interchange) using the principles and incorporating the eight core competencies of Supply Chain Synthesis into the electronic ("e-") relationship.

Five Supporting Technologies. To enhance SCS communications: Direct Link, LANs, WANs, VPNs, and EDI.

Flexibility. The ability to handle a variety of manufacturing requirements without alteration.

Global Supply Chain Vision. Must motivate employees and trading partners to view the world as their supplier through techniques designed to minimize and eliminate resistance to change, cultural biases, and stereotypes.

Holistic. Concerned with the entire system (i.e., supply chain) rather than the analysis of each part.

Integrated 3 PL providers. Outgrowth of a contract or for-hire logistics service, supplementing their services with other vendors' service offerings.

Integration. The seamless incorporation of processes, resources, and technologies into an organization or supply chain for higher functionality and advantage.

Inventory Design. Should be done with an eye to inventory reduction, inventory accuracy across the supply chain, and the effective combination of push and pull systems.

Joint Venture. When two companies form a separate entity with joint ownership to pursue a specific business objective.

Lean manufacturing. Based on the Toyota Production System; a series of flexible processes that enable product manufacture at a lower cost.

Linearity. The way knowledge progresses in SCM, from one link to another then to another; in SCS, knowledge transfer occurs through the supply chain simultaneously, typically through inexpensive electronic means (e.g., the Internet).

Link Optimization. The crux of SCM, whereby the health of the supply chain in aggregate is often sacrificed for the good of the individual link.

Logistics (traditional). Focused on internal coordination of materials management, materials flow, and physical distribution of finished goods.

Maintainability. The requirement for 24/7 uptime of equipment, enabled through preventive and predictive maintenance.

Management by Fad (MBF). The reactive selection of "Band-Aid" type approaches to improvement that only enable organizations to perform the wrong functions even more efficiently.

Manufacturing Synthesis. Lean, agile, cellular manufacturing that is a time-based approach to BTO and a streamlined approach to achieving speed; a core competency of SCS.

Merger/Acquisition. When companies lose their independence to become one corporate entity.

Modularity. The ability to expand or contract manufacturing volume without process alteration.

Network Design. Combines information technology with responsive, efficient, and effective manufacturing and distribution operations with a focus on reducing the number of DCs while being mindful of the type of products, range and volume of products, the level of service required, and the number and type of customers.

No Boundaries. The point where the supply chain has seamlessness in information, communication, and functionality; when it effectively becomes one entity rather than a series of links.

Non-asset-based 3PL. Focus on management and technological issues associated with providing logistics services; also known as management-based 3PL

Partnerships. The understanding—whether contractually bound or not—that sharing information openly, communicating requirements extensively, and involving alliances early in processes will provide competitive advantage and strength to an organization; a core competency of SCS.

Peak-to-Peak. Whereby an organization views itself as successful, but never successful enough; the process of continuously improving because the perception is that even though you're winning, you're still the underdog; a core competency of SCS.

Pipeline. The best way to physically depict a supply chain.

Postponement. The process of delaying customization (e.g., kitting, packaging, and labeling) until the product is received at a warehouse.

Predictive Maintenance (PdM). Anticipation of potential problems through system self-assessment and scheduling.

Preventive Maintenance (PM). Minimization of future problems through continuous checking and repair.

Proactive. The capacity to spot and troubleshoot problems before they become crises.

Process. An open-ended methodology that allows for continuous improvement.

Pull Distribution. Giving all distribution control to the customer (i.e., through ordering) rather than to the supplier.

Push Distribution. Giving all distribution control to the supplier rather than to the customer; based on forecasting.

Reactive. The traditional approach to uncertainty, also known as firefighting; trying to solve the crisis that arose from a problem when everyone is panicking.

Reliability. The demand for 24/7 uptime of equipment.

Remedy Management. Increasing the understanding of the positive effects of change and the negative effects of not changing.

Resilience The ability to absorb and adapt to Change. If the speed of change is greater than one's resilience, the individual cannot succeed.

Reverse Distribution. The task of recovering packaging and shipping materials and backhauling them to a central collection point for recycling.

Roundtable. A facilitated opportunity for suppliers and customers to share ideas about products and markets interactively, query existing beliefs, and uncover new opinions.

SCS Asset Management. Enables employees within the supply chain to share information about asset-specific data, procedures, and methods.

SCS Benchmark Assessment. A nine-point critical examination of how SCS is viewed by all partners and by the ultimate customer and is therefore a measure of the health of the supply chain in question.

SCS Business Plan. A multi-year, macro-level business plan that will serve as the requirements definition for the future of the supply chain.

SCS Communication. Simultaneous, instantaneous, and multi-directional to allow all supply chain partners to work at the same time rather than sequentially.

SCS Communication Team. Ensures and assures that everyone in the supply chain has a clear understanding of the SCS Model of Success, the status of teams, and the status of SCS.

SCS Demand Planning. Uses the Internet as the means for linking all customers, suppliers, and distributors in the supply chain so that they may collaborate.

SCS Event Planning. Monitors and controls events that impact supply and demand—promotion, competitive strategies, profitability, and sales volumes.

SCS Improvement Teams. Focus on incremental and continuous improvement in the areas defined in the process of prioritizing SCS opportunities for improvement

SCS Inventory Planning. Has extensive simulation capabilities, automated rules-driven analysis, and time-phased support. These elements help manufacturers and distributors reduce inventory costs while still meeting all customer requirements—even when they vary by product, group, or other criteria.

SCS Manufacturing Management. Accepts data forecasts, costs, and planning information from supply chain planning systems. It then balances the information with shop floor activities.

SCS Manufacturing Planning. A constraints-based planning that balances manufacturing processes and resources with demand priorities and supply chain objectives, which in turn simplify and accelerate the creation of long-range strategic capacity plans, tactical master production schedules, and operational schedules on the plant level.

SCS Order Management. Validates and prioritizes customer orders so that they may be processed as quickly and then prioritizes them for dissemination to the manufacturing, warehousing, and transportation systems

SCS Replenishment Planning. An advanced continuous replenishment strategy that uses the Internet for collaboration as well as extensive EDI support for automatic ordering, replenishment, invoicing, and shipping

SCS Steering Team. Created from the top level of the supply chain partners' organizations, this is the team that will be defining the direction the supply chain will be taking to achieve SCS.

SCS Transportation Management. Ability to track shipment inefficiencies, unnecessary costs, and excess labor through automation to handle load tendering, shipment documentation and confirmation, shipment status, and even freight auditing and payment.

SCS Transportation Planning. Generates shipping plans that balance network design, customer satisfaction design, and transportation design requirements. It considers the carriers, costs, transit time, and options that will satisfy the transportation design identified in the supply chain design process.

SCS Warehouse Management. Increases shipping and inventory accuracy by maximizing the flow of information and materials through the warehouse.

Selective Operability. The ability to function in segments without degradation of the aggregate system.

Siloism. The organization's focus on self-improvement, often at the expense of improvement of the entire supply chain.

Strategic Alliance. When companies work together to pursue a specific, single-focused business objective.

Strategic Initiatives. Center on establishing objectives and implementing continuous improvement recommendations to achieve performance excellence.

Strategic Planning. The development of future organizational requirements for a specific planning horizon.

Supply Chain Design. Comprised of network design, inventory design, transportation design, and customer satisfaction design.

Supply Chain Management (SCM). The approach to link optimization that takes organizations beyond traditional logistics but not to the competitive advantages offered by Supply Chain Synthesis.

Supply Chain Execution. The actual, physical movement and accounting of products through the supply chain.

Supply Chain Planning. A collaborative process that is comprised of demand planning, event planning, inventory planning, replenishment planning, manufacturing planning, and transportation planning; the information required to place the right product at the right location at the right time.

Supply Chain Synthesis (SCS). The holistic, continuous improvement process that seeks to optimize the entire supply chain rather than each link through the maximization of its eight core competencies.

Tactical Initiatives. Center on fixing problems and resolving issues that detract from operational excellence.

Third-party logistics (3PL). Using another organization's space, resources, processes, and/or technology to perform all or part of the logistics function.

Total Operations. The blending of all functional areas in a facility to create a highly efficient and effective organization; these functional areas are warehousing, distribution, manufacturing, maintenance, quality, systems, and organizational excellence; a core competency of SCS.

Trading Partner Agreement (TPA). A formal contract that fills in the blanks left by existing contract laws, rules of evidence, and issues of liability.

Transportation Design. Looks beyond internal transportation needs to all supply chain transportation needs and develops an ideal system based on transportation models.

Uncertainty. The byproduct of lack of discipline and control; SCS environments increase discipline and control through communication of processes and standards.

Upgradeability. The ability to gracefully incorporate changes and advances in equipment, systems, methodologies, and technologies.

Vision. Includes expressions of optimism, hope, excellence, ideals, and possibilities for your supply chain for tomorrow.

Winning Manufacturing. Utilizes the best practices of lean, cellular, and agile manufacturing and is a journey of continuous improvement, addressing everything from product development to marketing and employing a philosophy of dynamic consistency.

WORKS CONSULTED

BOOKS

Bennis, W. *On Becoming a Leader.* Phoenix: Perseus, 1994.

Dell, Michael and Catherine Fredman. *Direct from Dell: Strategies That Revolutionized an Industry.* New York: HarperBusiness, 1999.

Davis, Stanley M. *Blur: The Speed of Change in the Connected Economy.* Reading, Mass.: Addison-Wesley, 1998.

Tompkins, James A. and Dale Harmelink, eds. *The Distribution Management Handbook.* Boston, Mass.: McGraw Hill, 1994.

Tompkins, James A. and Jerry D. Smith, eds. *The Warehouse Management Handbook.* Raleigh, NC: Tompkins Press, 1998.

Tompkins, James A. *Winning Manufacturing: The How-To Book of Successful Manufacturing.* Norcross, Ga: Industrial Engineering and Management Press, 1989.

Tompkins, Jim. *Revolution: Take Charge Strategies for Business Success.* Raleign, NC: Tompkins Press, 1998.

MONOGRAPHS

Tompkins Associates, Inc. *Achieving Logistics Excellence through Supply Chain Synthesis.* Raleigh, NC: Tompkins Press, 1999.

_____. *Crossdocking in the Future.* Raleigh, NC: Tompkins Press, 1998.

_____. *Customer Service is a Smile, Right?* Raleigh, NC: Tompkins Press, 1996.

_____. *Designing a Distribution Network.* Raleigh, NC: Tompkins Press, 1998.

_____. *The Ins and Outs of Cycle Counting,* Raleigh, NC: Tompkins Press, 1997.

_____. *Inventory: the Unwanted Asset.* Raleigh, NC: Tompkins Press, 1997.

_____. *The Journey to Warehousing Excellence.* Raleigh, NC: Tompkins Press, Tompkins Press, 1999.

_____. *Warehouse Management Technologies.* Raleigh, NC: Tompkins Press, 1998.

ARTICLES

A Master Class in Radical Change," *Fortune* (13 December 1993).

"E-Commerce Update." *Distribution Channels* (June 1999).

"Overheard." *Selling Power* (October 1999).

"Quote of the Week." *Information Week* (18 October 1999).

"Re-engineering the Supply Chain: One Company's Strategy." *Industry Week Solutions Guide* (October 1999).

"Software Tools: The Quick and the Dead." *Modern Materials Handling* (October 1999).

"Survey: Top Performers Cut SCM Costs to 4 Percent of Sales." *Modern Distribution Management* (21 October 1999).

"Up Front." *Logistics* (February 1998).

"UPS Group to Help Ford Streamline New Car Delivery." *The News and Observer* (3 February 2000).

Allnoch, Allen. "Efficient Supply Chain Practices Mean Big Savings to Leading Manufacturers." *IIE Solutions* (July 1997).

Anderson, David L., Frank F. Britt, and Donavon J. Favre. "The Seven Principles of Supply Chain Management." *Supply Chain Management Review* (Spring 1997).

Baer, Tony. "E-business Transforms Manufacturing." *Manufacturing Systems* (July 1999).

Bylinsky, Gene. "For Sale: Japanese Plants in the U.S." *Fortune* (February 2000).

Bradley, Peter. "Logistics Product." *Logistics* (July 1998).

Brooks, Rick. "Alienating Customers Isn't Always a Bad Idea, Many Firms Discover." *New York Times* (7 January 1999).

Brown, Stuart F. "Wresting New Wealth from the Supply Chain." *Fortune* (9 November 1998).

Cook, James Aaron. "Tool Time." *Logistics Tech* (March 1999).

Coronna, Mark. "E-Commerce to E-Business." *Inbound Logistics* (September 1999).

Fine, Charles H. "The Ultimate Core Competency." *Fortune* (29 March 1999).

Gentry, Connie. "The Price of Progress: Affordable E-Commerce." *Inbound Logistics* (November 1998).

Gilmore, Dan and James A. Tompkins. "Get Me a Real WMS." *IDS* (March 1999).

Gilmore, Dan and James A. Tompkins. "The Value of Logistics Is on the Rise." *IDS* (November 1999).

Godin, Patty. "A New Scheduling Regime." *IIE Solutions* (June 1999).

Godin, Patty. "Growing a Global Economy." *Competitive Edge* (Winter 1999).

Gould, Janet. "Technology Focus." *IDS* (June 1999).

Gould, Janet. "The Internet Turns the Manufacturing Paradigm Upside Down." *IDS* (June 1999).

Grackin, Ann. "Opportunities Flourish in the e-World." *Competitive Edge* (Winter 1999).

Handfield, Robert B. and Daniel R. Krause. "Think Globally, Source Locally." *Supply Chain Management Review* (Winter 1999).

Hewitt, Fred. "Global Pipeline Management: Beyond SCM." *Supply Chain Management Review* (Winter 1999).

Hoffman, Kurt C. "The Vision: Suppliers, Manufacturers, Retailers Collaborating as One." *Global Sites and Logistics* (June 1998).

Kahl, Steven J. "What's the Value of Supply Chain Software?" *Supply Chain Management Review* (Winter 1999).

Kilbane, Doris. "The Secrets to EDI's Staying Power." *Automatic ID News* (October 1999).

Kirsner, Scott. "The Customer Experience." *Net Company* (Fall 1999).

Knill, Bernie. "IT Strikes Back: The Sequel." *Material Handling Engineering* (October 1998).

Krass, Louis John. "Building a Business Case for Supply Chain Technology." *Supply Chain Management Review* (Winter 1999).

LaLonde, Bernard J. . "The Quest for Supply Chain Integration." *Supply Chain Management Review* (Winter 1999).

Landry, John T. "Supply Chain Management: The Case for Alliances." *Harvard Business Review* (November/December 1998).

Laseter, Timothy M. "Integrating the Supply Web." *Supply Chain Management Review* (Winter 1999).

Leon, Mark. "Brushing Up on Supply Chain." *Consulting Magazine* (November 1999).

Magretta, Joan. "The Power of Virtual Integration: An Interview with Dell Computer's Michael Dell." *Harvard Business Review* (March/April 1998).

Malone, Robert. "An Alliance for Progress." *Inbound Logistics* (June 1999).

Marien, Edward J. "Demand Planning and Sales Forecasting: A Supply Chain Essential." *Supply Chain Management Review* (Winter 1999).

McManus, John. "A Weather Watch." *American Demographics* (October 1999).

Olsen, Robert L. "Building a Better Supply Chain." *Competitive Edge* (Spring 1999).

Olsen, Robert L., "The Internet May Not Be the End of the Road for EDI." *Frozen Food Age* (October, 1999)

Parker, Kevin. "New Fundamentals." *Manufacturing Systems* (July 1999).

Pascale, Richard, Mark Millemann, and Linda GIOJA. "Changing the Way We Change." *Harvard Business Review* (November/ December 1997).

Pavis, Theta. "Digging for Data and Dollars." *Warehousing Management* (November/December 1999).

Purkiss, Mark. "Paperless is More: Warehousing Today and into the 21st Century." *Automatic ID News Europe* (September 1999).

Quinn, Franis J. "The Payoff!" *Logistics Management* (December 1997).

Robertson, Robert. "Take That One: Pick-to-Light Systems Made Easy." *Materials Management and Distribution* (August 1999).

Salcedo, Simon and Ann Grackin, "The e-Value Chain." *Supply Chain Management Review* (Winter 2000).

Schlegel, Gregory L. "Supply Chain Optimization: A Practitioner's Perspective." *Supply Chain Management Review* (Winter 1999).

Sparks, Debra. "Special Report: Partners." *Business Week* (25 October 1999).

Stein, Tom. "Agile Anywhere Takes Supply chains Online." *Information Week* (21 June 1999).

Swanton, Bill. "Managing the Change That E-Business Brings." *Software Strategies* (November/Decmeber 1999).

Tompkins, James A. "Demand Flow Leadership." *EC World* (February 1997).

_____. "Earnings Across the Supply Chain." *Supply Chain Technology New* (September/October 1999).

_____. "Enhancing the Warehouse's Role through Customization." *Warehousing Education and Research Council Special Report* (February 1997).

_____. "Who's Walking Who?" *Automatic ID News Europe (October 1999).*

_____. "Supply Chain Flow: James Tompkins on Supply Chain Synthesis." *Supply Chain Flow* (August 1998).

Tompkins, James A., Bernie Knill, and Tom Andel, "Time to Rise Above Supply Chain Management." *Supply Chain Flow* (Supplement, October 1998).

Tompkins, Jim and Forsyth Alexander. "e- Comes of Age." *Competitive Edge* (Winter 1999).

Trommer, Diane. "As 'Build to Order' Fires Up the PC Business, Can the Supply Chain Stand the Heat?" *Electronic Buyer's News* (15 December 1997).

Vasilash, Gary S. "The Real World." *Automotive Manufacturing and Production* (July 1998).

Weil, Marty. "Some Assembly Required." *Manufacturing Systems* (August 1999).

White, Gregory L. "How GM, Ford Think Web Can Make Splash on the Factory Floor." *Wall Street Journal* (9 November 1999).

WEB SITES AND WEB ARTICLES

"Logility Announces i-Commerce Strategy." http://www.logility.com (27 July 1999).

"The Road from Craft Work to Agile Manufacturing." http://www.detroitnews.com (28 December 1999).

Aiken, Joy. "Intel Corporation." http://www.hoovers.com (15 November 1999).

Bartlett's Quotes Online. http://www.bartleby.com.

Carbone, James. "High-Tech Buyers See Tidal Wave of Opportunity." http://www.manufacturing.net/magazine/mmh/ (17 June 1999).

Frank's Creative Quotes from Famous People. http://www.bemorecreative.com.
http://www.cpfr.org

Milligan, Brian. "Despite Attempts to Break Them, Functional Silos Live On." http://www.manufacturing.net/magazine/purchasing/ (4 November 1999).

Modern Materials Handling Online. http://www.manufacturing.net/magazine/mmh/.

Purchasing Online. http://www.manufacturing.net/magazine/purchasing/.

Stedman, Craig. "Some Firms Use EDI Links to Trade Data, But Turn to Web for Real-time Planning. http://www.computerworld.com (15 November 1999).

INDEX

F

G

190, 212, 217, 223, 231-231, 234
  Gomez, Lefty 63
  Gould, Janet 15
  Government involvement 122
  Gross domestic product (GDP) 5, 125
  Group technology 106, 254
  Guiding Principles 214, 221-222

H

Harmony 83, 85, 113
Harvard Business Review 22, 25, 63
Heineken 177
Historical trends 175
Holism 30-31
Holistic 2, 20, 35, 53, 58, 82, 256, 261
Hood, Ray 121
HTML 165, 171, 176
Human Resources 235
Huxley, Aldous 76
Hybrid push/pull system 121, 141, 145
Hyundai 168

I

Implementation i, 28, 103, 124, 131,
132, 133, 135, 136, 137, 182, 185, 202,
216, 217, 220, 224, 253
  Implemented performance 231
  Imports 136
  Incremental analysis 237
  Industrial Revolution 42
  Information ii, iv, 3, 6, 7, 11, 14, 16, 17,
18, 20, 21, 22, 25, 30, 37, 39, 55, 56, 60,
69, 70, 78, 79, 83, 87, 88, 90, 97, 99, 103,
105, 120, 122, 124, 128, 129, 130, 131,
136, 138, 139, 151, 154, 159, 160, 163,
166, 167, 168, 169, 170, 173, 174, 175,
176, 184, 185, 187, 189, 194, 195, 196,
200, 203, 204, 205, 206, 212, 217, 225,
234, 255, 257, 259, 260, 261
  Information Superhighway iii
  Information Systems 11, 16, 17, 60,
121, 122, 125, 126, 164, 166, 173, 200,
204, 206
  Information Technology (IT) 12, 126,
132, 144, 164, 170, 177, 203, 257
    Initiatives i, 34, 156, 171, 187, 205,

206, 220, 221, 228, 261, 262
  Innovation i, 30, 56, 59, 75, 82, 90,
151, 152, 153, 188, 189, 198, 205, 216,
220
  Insider trading 37
  Integrated (3PL) providers 138
  Integration ii, iv, 2, 3, 8, 11, 20, 21, 22,
24, 23, 28, 29, 34, 35, 42, 50, 51, 52, 53,
54, 56, 57, 58, 59, 82, 87, 88, 102, 105,
117, 153, 159, 164, 165, 173, 176, 188,
189, 192, 196, 204, 206, 220, 224, 225,
232, 236, 256
  Intel 74, 75
  Intellectual capital 46
  Interactions 29, 154, 155
  Interdependence 60, 166
  Interface standards 224, 236
  Intermodal services 136
  International Pre-distribution Process
120
  Internet iii, 6, 7, 12, 16, 17, 18, 25, 29,
39, 48, 57, 76, 147, 161, 164, 165, 166,
167, 168, 169, 171, 172, 173, 176, 177,
180, 187, 189, 191, 201, 204, 205, 206,
207, 255, 256, 259, 260
  Intimacy 150, 159, 237
  Intranets 16, 171
  Inventory iii, 2, 7, 12, 21, 23, 33, 34,
37, 39, 40, 45, 47, 49, 58, 59, 74, 83, 84,
85, 99, 103, 104, 108, 110, 113, 114, 115,
116, 119, 120, 121, 123, 125, 127, 128,
129, 136, 137, 138, 140, 141, 145, 152,
163, 164, 166, 167, 170, 175, 177, 181,
182, 183, 185, 187, 188, 189, 190, 192,
193, 194, 195, 205, 220, 223, 225, 226,
233, 234, 235, 236, 255, 256, 259, 261
  Inventory design 180, 182, 183, 190,
256, 261
  Inventory planning 36, 180, 187, 188,
190, 225, 259, 261
  Invoices 91, 130, 167, 170

J

Java 172, 172, 176
JavaScript 176
Joint venture 151, 256
Jordan, Michael 55-56
Just-in-Time (JIT) iii, 36, 114, 227

K

Kanban 103
Key performance indicators (KPIs) 196
Kickbacks 37
Kissinger, Henry 72
Knowledge 5, 43, 46, 50, 56, 59, 78, 105, 145, 204, 205, 206, 213, 216, 227, 253, 256
Knowledge management 204
Kuzu 147

L

LANs 16, 169, 255
Latin American markets 200
Layout and equipment 128
Leadership 3, 68, 76, 77, 79, 82, 86, 109, 122, 125, 155, 156, 157, 170, 210, 213, 224, 227, 231, 254
Lead-time 110, 177
Lean manufacturing 102, 103, 104, 105, 233, 253, 256
Less-than truckload (LTL) 140
Lincoln, Abraham 73
Linearity 57, 256
Liz Claiborne 170
Load plan 192
Logility 176-177
Logistics 8, 12, 13, 34, 38, 49, 51, 52, 53, 54, 58, 59, 65, 75, 82, 83, 84, 85, 93, 119, 120, 121, 123, 138, 142, 145, 153, 181, 182, 186, 194, 195, 204, 253, 256, 257, 261, 262
Logistics magazine 51-52
Lot/expiration date control 194
Lot sizes 81, 87, 108, 110, 114, 140, 233, 234, 236

M

Machine Age 42
Maintainability 20, 135, 256
Maintenance 8, 23, 24, 82, 83, 84, 85, 87, 106, 113, 129, 132, 140, 165, 172, 193, 196, 197, 234, 235, 256, 258, 262
Maintenance scheduling 24

Management-based (3PL) providers 138
Management by Fad (MBF) 8, 257
Manufacturing iii, 3, 5, 8, 11, 12, 13, 14, 15, 22, 23, 25, 26, 27, 28, 34, 35, 38, 39, 42, 43, 70, 81, 82, 83, 84, 85, 86, 87, 98, 101, 102, 104, 105, 106, 107, 108, 109, 110, 111, 113, 114, 115, 116, 117, 119, 123, 135, 137, 139, 140, 141, 145, 148, 179, 180, 181, 182, 184, 186, 187-189, 190, 191, 192, 193, 196, 204, 207, 211, 215, 223, 225, 231, 232, 233, 234, 235, 236, 237, 253, 254, 255, 257, 260, 261, 262
Manufacturing Assembly Pilot (MAP) 34
Manufacturing Execution Systems (MESs) 87
Manufacturing planning 180, 187, 188, 191, 192, 196, 260, 261
Manufacturing management 108, 180, 193, 196, 237, 260
Manufacturing synthesis 61, 86, 87, 101, 102, 106, 108, 109, 111, 114, 116, 117, 178, 182, 215, 224, 225, 254, 257
Manugistics iii
Marino, Dan 142
Market share 30, 70, 85, 110, 148, 149, 220
Marketing component 58
Martinez, Arthur 65
Master Production Schedule 191, 260
Master Trading Partner Agreement 203
Material flow 20, 38, 52, 103, 115, 139, 182, 194, 235
Material handling 3, 21, 42, 43, 58, 83, 87, 106, 110, 124, 132, 134, 182, 193, 233, 235
Material tracking and control 235
Materials management 52, 256
Maximized discounts 193
Maximum value 2, 40
Mayer, Irv 73
Merchandising 65
Merck, 185
Mercosur (South American Common Market) 17
Mergers and acquisitions 23
Merrill Lynch 38
Mexico 17, 203
Microsoft 17

N

P

S

T

U

V

W

X, Y, Z

ABOUT TOMPKINS PRESS

Established in 1997, Tompkins Press is dedicated to providing readers with the latest and most up-to-date information on Total Operations through leading-edge publications that share our experiences and expertise. Our desire to help others achieve Peak-to-Peak Performance and maintain a competitive advantage in today's ever-changing environment is the driving force behind our success. Our most recent publications include:

- *Warehouse Management Handbook - Second Edition*
- *REVOLUTION: Take Charge Strategies for Business Success*
- *REVOLUTION: Take Charge Strategies for Business Success, Audio Edition*
- *Goose Chase: Capturing the Energy of Change in Logistics*
- *Goose Chase: Capturing the Energy of Change in Logistics, Audio Edition*
- *No Boundaries: Moving Beyond Supply Chain Management*
- *No Boundaries: Moving Beyond Supply Chain Management, Audio Edition*

For more information about Tompkins Press, contact tompkinspress@tompkinsinc.com.

About Tompkins Associates

From our beginning over 25 years ago, Tompkins has offered clients long-term solutions that accommodate companies' changing needs and provide the foundation for future growth. With an emphasis on integrated solutions, Tompkins' Total Operations expertise provides the understanding that can guide companies to operational excellence. Tompkins provides expertise in Supply Chain Synthesis, warehousing, systems implementations, material handling, facilities planning, manufacturing, workplace leadership, team-building, construction services, maintenance, quality and organizational excellence.

Tompkins Associates understands back-end operations. Tompkins' expertise in order fulfillment and supply chain systems will help clients provide the service they need to satisfy their customers. Only Tompkins Associates does this at the speed of "e."

With its corporate headquarters located in Raleigh, NC, Tompkins Associates has offices throughout the United States in Atlanta, GA; Chicago, IL; Irvine, CA; Allentown, PA; Dallas, TX and Raleigh, NC. Tompkins also has offices in Warwick, UK, Toronto, Canada and Buenos Aires, Argentina.

No Boundaries